PRAISE FOR

THE SINGLE M♡M'S DEVOTIONAL

The Single Mom's Devotional is an encouraging buoy in the swirling waters of single parenting. With Christ at the center of these 52 weeks of devotions, Carol wraps her experiences with encouragement, practical insight, reflection and Scripture.

SANDRA P. ALDRICH
Author, *From One Single Mother to Another*

Single moms are dear to God's heart, and He longs to comfort and care for them. Carol's book is a love letter from Jesus to these precious daughters of the king. I pray they will find His grace in these pages.

PETE BRISCOE
Senior Pastor, Bent Tree Bible Fellowship

When my wife died, I too, began the gut-wrenching journey of being a single parent. It was brutal, but God was faithful. My friend Carol Floch and her wise words are a spiritual balm for the aching soul. Don't just read this devotional, but also ingest it, live it and let the truths of God's Word transform you.

ROB BUGH
Senior Pastor, Wheaton Bible Church

This amazing devotional is open, honest and vulnerable. It is written out of the author's own pain, disillusionment and recovery as a single mom. It is also solidly rooted in Scripture—Carol's main source of strength. We highly recommend it!

GENE AND ELAINE GETZ
Pastor Emeritus, Chase Oaks Church/Director, Center for Church Renewal

"Thoughtful," "engaging" and "wise" are three words I would use to describe Carol Floch. Her contemplative work is biblically based and serves not only to inspire but also to strengthen the reader. Carol is a gifted writer, and God has equipped her with a powerful message to share with single moms and their kids.

KAROL LADD
Author, *The Power of a Positive Mom*

This thoughtful, beautifully written devotional is infused with Scripture through and through. Carol gently uncovers the deepest needs of women who are parenting alone and also suggests ways that they can help nurture their children. *The Single Moms Devotional* helps me even now redeem my own challenging years as a single parent.

DR. SCOTTIE MAY
Assistant Professor of Christian Formation and Ministry, Wheaton College

In *The Single Mom's Devotional*, Carol Floch not only tells her own story of experiencing the crushing disappointment of divorce but also shows how relying on the grace and loyal love of God can redeem children and their grieving mothers from regret and despair. I hope this book finds its way into the hands of every single mom who needs the assurance that God is not finished with her.

DR. E. ANDREW MCQUITTY
Senior Pastor, Irving Bible Church

Carol Floch tenderly guides single moms through heartbreak and loss to a place of security and hope. Her compassionate insight and practical wisdom will encourage and strengthen single moms along their journey as parents.

MARILYN MEBERG
Counselor, Author and Women of Faith Speaker

Carol Floch knows what it is like to have your world knocked over through the upheaval of divorce. She also knows what it means to have God enter her upside-down world and show her how to hang on through the disaster. Carol opens her life and God's Word to guide and encourage those whose lives have been overturned by divorce.

DR. DEBORAH NEWMAN
Minister to Women, Christ Church

In *The Single Mom's Devotional*, Carol Floch offers hope and refreshment to single moms and reminds them to be passionately committed to their two most important priorities: (1) pursuing undivided devotion to Christ, and (2) loving and disciplining their children. This book will provide a daily rock of security for every single mom who reads and applies its words.

GARY SPRAGUE
Founder and President, Center for Single-Parent Family Ministry

A Book of 52 Practical and Encouraging Devotions

THE SINGLE MOM'S DEVOTIONAL

CAROL FLOCH

Regal

From Gospel Light
Ventura, California, U.S.A.

Published by Regal
From Gospel Light
Ventura, California, U.S.A.
www.regalbooks.com
Printed in the U.S.A.

Library of Congress Cataloging-in-Publication Data
Floch, Carol.
The single mom's devotional : a book of 52 practical and encouraging devotions /
Carol Floch.
p. cm.
ISBN 978-0-8307-5161-7 (trade paper)
1. Single mothers—Prayers and devotions.
2. Christian women—Prayers and devotions.
I. Title.
BV4847.F56 2010
242'.645—dc22
2009035376

1 2 3 4 5 6 7 8 9 10 / 16 15 14 13 12 11 10

Rights for publishing this book outside the U.S.A. or in non-English languages
are administered by Gospel Light Worldwide, an international not-for-profit ministry.
For additional information, please visit www.glww.org, email info@glww.org, or write to
Gospel Light Worldwide, 1957 Eastman Avenue, Ventura, CA 93003, U.S.A.

TO MOM AND DAD,

WHO TAUGHT ME THE CENTRALITY OF THE CROSS

OF JESUS CHRIST TO ALL OF LIFE;

and

TO MY CHILDREN,

BETHANY JOY, ROBIN AND EMILY.

YOU ARE MY PRECIOUS GIFTS FROM GOD,

LIVING EXAMPLES OF HIS AMAZING GRACE.

I LOVE YOU WITH ALL MY HEART.

CONTENTS

Foreword *by Karol Ladd* 8

Preface 10

1. Fear of the Future 15
2. Heartache 19
3. Forgetfulness 23
4. Self-worth 27
5. Shame 31
6. Redefining Life 35
7. Identity 39
8. Acceptance 43
9. Isolation 47
10. Loneliness 51
11. Empowerment 55
12. Service 59
13. Trust 63
14. Disappointment 67
15. Discouragement 71
16. Vulnerability 75
17. Insecurity 79
18. Fear 83
19. Struggle 87
20. Waiting 91
21. Fellowship 95
22. Pride 99
23. Inadequacy 103
24. Facing Limitations 107
25. Injustice 110

26. Freedom from Guilt...115

27. Forgiving the Unforgivable 119

28. Broken Relationships..123

29. Starting Over...127

30. Contentment...131

31. A Painful Past...135

32. God Uses Everything...139

33. Loss...143

34. Spiritual Healing..147

35. Chasing Wind...151

36. Running on Empty..155

37. Removing the Idols 159

38. Offering Myself 163

39. Worship..167

40. Relinquishing Control...171

41. A Place of Surrender..175

42. The Battle of Self...179

43. Worry 183

44. Dependence...187

45. Rest...191

46. Reliance 195

47. Praise 199

48. Daily Events...203

49. Despair...207

50. Purpose..211

51. Obedience 215

52. Embracing Your Place Near His Altar..................219

Acknowledgments...223

❧ FOREWORD ❧

by Karol Ladd

Do you remember the first day when you added the title of "Mom" to your life? Along with new and sometimes challenging responsibilities, there was also a love that developed deep within your soul, which few words can describe. Being a mom is filled with delight, mixed with a little fear and a small dose of stretching us beyond our comfort zone. If we are going to be quite honest, motherhood isn't all that easy. Add to the mix parenting alone, and the role of motherhood can become downright overwhelming.

When it comes to single parenting, you are not alone. There are two different messages in that one statement. You are not alone, because there are many other moms who are walking down the same path as you. The number of single moms in our nation has dramatically increased over the last 30 years. You must admit there is a small amount of comfort in knowing that you are not the only one who is traveling this path of parenting alone. But most importantly, you are not alone because there is a God who loves you and welcomes you to turn to Him for guidance, comfort and help. This is a book that points you toward His loving care and walks with you down a path of finding your security and strength in Him.

The Single Mom's Devotional offers you a resource of biblical wisdom and comfort to your soul. Written by a mom who has walked down the road of single parenting herself, this devotional will meet you right where you are. In her penetrating yet relational style, Carol Floch opens up God's Word to you in a fresh and meaningful way as a single mom. Her personal examples from her own journey serve as a rich backdrop to the beauty that is illuminated from God's Word. In each of the 52 devotionals you will find truth for yourself, and you will also discover important truths to share with your children.

Carol not only speaks and writes with wisdom gleaned from God's Word; she also lives it. I have been a close friend of Carol's for over 10 years and have watched her apply God's grace, love and wisdom in her daily life. More importantly, I have seen her encourage her children's growth and dependence on the Lord. Without a doubt, Carol has found her strength in the Lord as she has raised her three precious daughters as a single parent.

This devotional is unique, because it is written for you, specifically as a single mom. Carol has included truth from God's Word, personal application, quotes from godly men and women and important ways to enrich your children's relationship with the Lord. Many single parents feel alone, but the blessing is that you have resources like this to help you along your journey. You can use this devotional for your own personal spiritual growth or you can join with other single moms to learn from God's Word together. Either way, you are sure to find joy and strength from the stories, examples and biblical wisdom found in these pages.

What is the key to raising children on your own as a Christian? If I were to put it into one word, I would say "abide." Jesus said, "I am the vine; you are the branches. If a man remains in me and I in him, he will bear much fruit; apart from me you can do nothing" (John 15:5). This devotional draws you into a place of abiding in Him. The intent is to help you find a place close to His altar and abide in His presence in your everyday life. I know that your personal life and your parenting will be enriched as you draw close to God and enjoy a very real and vibrant relationship with Him. May God use this book to encourage you as a mom and help you feel His warm embrace as His beloved daughter.

Karol Ladd
Author, *The Power of a Positive Mom*

PREFACE

When my sisters and I played house as children, we would argue about who had to play the dad. It never occurred to us to have a mom and kids without a dad as we acted out our childhood fantasies. After all, little girls don't dream of someday becoming single moms. But for a growing sorority of women, childhood dreams turn into nightmares, and this unforeseen reality becomes part of their script—an unrehearsed part they must somehow successfully pull off before a live audience, their children.

The day I realized my marriage was going to end in divorce, I wept uncontrollably. My losses were innumerable, but my children's losses were incalculable. I had hoped to wake up from the nightmare of marital separation to a happily-ever-after restoration, not the outcome of divorce.

But what about my children? I asked the Lord, shuddering at the long-term impact of divorce. *Where will their security be?* Even as I wept, the words "Psalm 84" began quietly but persistently niggling at the back of my mind. Somewhat perplexed, I finally reached for my Bible and began reading the unfamiliar passage through my tears: "How lovely is your dwelling place, O LORD . . ." when I came to verses 3-4, I caught my breath: "Even the sparrow has found a home, and the swallow a nest for herself, where she may have her young—a place near your altar, O LORD Almighty, my King and my God. Blessed are those who dwell in your house; they are ever praising you." I read the verses again and again, straining to discern the truth hidden in them. *Build your home at a place near my altar; I AM their security.* As I continued to read the psalm, He whispered more assurances to me. *Build your "nest" near my altar, and I will be your children's source of security, protection, provision, and blessing. I always have been, and I always will be.*

I realized that I had been hoping in neatly scripted outcomes for my children's (and my) wellbeing, not the Lord's constancy and sufficiency. Our lives were changing in uncontrollable ways, but God remained the same—in every confusing yesterday, in the heartache of today and in every unknown tomorrow. He would remain our faithful God!

That day, I resolved to intentionally nurture my family at a place near His altar—and to figure out what that meant on a day-to-day basis. I had been a Christian since my childhood. Bible stories, church involvement and Christian values stemming from my relationship with Christ were already woven into the fabric of our daily lives. Now I needed to find their relevance to the very painful path we were walking as a family. From the outset, nurturing my family at a place near His altar meant clinging to what I knew of God's character and His promises regardless of painful circumstances, and responding to His love through deliberate and sometimes difficult obedience, regardless of ambivalent feelings. It meant finding and claiming my sense of value, belonging and competence in Christ, the source of my true identity, and teaching my children to do the same. It meant intentionally putting my hand, and the hands of my children, in God's hand, day by day.

As the nightmare of divorce took on a life of its own—full of uncertainties and unpredictable outcomes—my heavenly Father gently prodded me: *Tend your nest; tend your nest.* Each day presented a tempting minefield of soul-traps—bitterness, resentment, self-pity, fear, anxiety, hatred, contempt, self-doubt, God-doubt—but I could not afford to go down that destructive path. Living at a place near His altar meant prayerfully keeping Christ's death on the cross for me in full view day by day, even hour to hour, to find grace and mercy for myself and to extend them to others. As I wrestled with a wounded reputation due to false rumors in my church and community, my true identity became more firmly anchored in Christ. My utter powerlessness pressed me to rely on God's all-powerfulness as I struggled to surrender outcomes for my children and me. "Surrendering outcomes" proved to be the most difficult yet most essential aspect of living at the foot of the cross, both then and now.

Two weeks after one particularly harrowing incident that completely altered the course of legal outcomes for my three daughters and me, I opened a gift from my sister. It was a framed photograph of a robin's nest holding four fragile eggs; below was the promise from Jeremiah 29:11: " 'For I know the plans that I have for you,' declares the LORD, 'plans for welfare and not for calamity to give you a future and a hope' " (*NASB*). I hung it in a prominent place in our home as a daily reminder of God's promises for me and my children.

Several months later, as my attorney filed a petition requesting permission (against all odds) to relocate to another state with my children, a robin industriously built her nest on the ledge of my sun porch window. Each day, this feathered friend served as God's visual aid, reminding me that our wellbeing hinged on God Himself as I intentionally depended on Him. *I am your source of security, protection, provision and blessing.*

One spring morning, I called to the children, "Look, the robin laid three eggs—one for each of you!" Several weeks later, on Mother's Day, we discovered three baby birds had hatched! During that time, the robin's vigilant care over her young reminded me to nurture my children with attentiveness despite stressful distractions, particularly as court-related issues were coming to a head. *Tend your nest; tend your nest. Trust the outcomes to Me.* By faith, I readied my house to sell so that we would be prepared to move, should we be given the opportunity.

Near the end of May, I asked the elders at my church to pray very specifically for permission to move; that afternoon, my attorney called to inform me that through a sudden reversal, permission was being granted! A few days later, after an appointment for finalizing the legal paperwork, I settled down to eat dinner with my children on the sun porch. We heard a rustling and looked up in time to see the baby birds take their first flight, never to return to the nest again. The details of our own move fell together in a rapid and amazing fashion over the next two months, bearing the fingerprints of God's intervention. Our "Red Sea" had parted, and we walked across on dry ground!

Eight years later and a thousand miles away, that same robin's nest sits cradled in a pair of large ceramic hands on my kitchen hutch, still providing a daily reminder: *Tend your nest; tend your nest. I am your source of security, protection, provision and blessing.* Through many trials and plenty of errors, the years have unfolded lesson upon lesson about living with my children at a place near His altar—centered on Him regardless of circumstances, surrendered to Him in all circumstances.

God's comforting invitation to this secure place near His altar stands in stark contrast to the loss of place experienced by single moms. Over the years, a growing sisterhood of "single mom" friendships has exposed the breadth of these losses: the awkwardness of feeling out of place; the insecurity or paralysis that accompanies not knowing their place; and a sense of inferiority and disgrace if they have been replaced. Frantic efforts to find their place by chasing a sense of significance or worth in relationships or the workplace can divert their attention from their children, who are often caught in the tailspin. In addition, single moms express a sense of powerlessness and grief as they observe the ramifications of loss of place experienced by their children, shuttled weekly between households.

The confusion from loss of place—playing out in their homes, in social relationships, in their participation in the church and even in their personal relationship with God—threatens to unravel the social and spiritual fibers that are deeply wired psychologically in them as women. For women, "place" carries a sense of security, belonging and safety—and that is God's reassuring invitation to single mothers at "a place near [His] altar."

What is the appeal of this "altar" where God invites the single mom to rebuild her life and nurture her young? From my background, an altar conjures up images of an austere, pristine place at the front of a vast cathedral, where children should not run and play, and people only speak in hushed tones—a place far removed from the daily hubbub of real life. Beautiful, maybe, but hardly warm and inviting, and certainly not a place to choose to live! I wondered why the notes in my *NIV Study Bible* indicate the psalmist *envied* the small birds nesting in the eaves of the temple that enjoyed "unhindered access" to the altar. To understand the psalmist's perspective, I embarked on an Old Testament "dig," and unearthed a wealth of insight about what the altar represented to the children of Israel.

The earliest biblical altars were built out of stones as memorials. When God "showed up" in an extraordinary way during the course of life, an altar was built to worship Him, remembering His name and celebrating His gracious intervention in their lives. The altar in the tabernacle, and later in the Temple, was the center of activity 24 hours a day, abuzz with the business of offerings and animal sacrifices. It was the meeting place between a holy God and His people, honoring a permanent, intimate, defining relationship. It reminded the people of God's unfailing love and faithfulness, their identity as His beloved people and their purpose as His chosen ones to bear His name and reveal His glory. The altar was a place of receiving forgiveness, acceptance and assurance. It was a place of experiencing redemption, reconciliation and restoration. It was a place of finding refuge and of giving thanks. It was a place of celebrating God's presence, His promises and His provision. The altar was a place where God offered His life to His people as they presented their offerings and their lives to Him.

The many facets of this unfolding picture of the altar foreshadowed the cross, where Jesus Christ, the Lamb of God, surrendered His life as a sacrifice for our sin. His death permanently opened the door for unhindered access to the throne of grace for all who seek God's forgiveness. "For Christ died for sins once for all, the righteous for the unrighteous, to bring you to God" (1 Peter 3:18). The cross is the altar where Christ settled accounts for all time on the most fundamental relationships and issues of life.

As such, the cross is the altar where you, as a single mom, are invited to come to terms daily with your relationship with God, your sense of personal identity, your relationships with others and your purpose and choices in life. The cross is the starting point of an intimate, covenant relationship; the secure place of identity and belonging as God's beloved; and a place of finding perspective and purpose in a confusing, fragile world. Living at a place near God's altar means daily staying tethered to the cross as the source of your identity, finding your true life in Christ and allowing for the outworking of Christ's life in yours as you nurture your children and navigate unpredictable relationships and outcomes. It is the place where you will find your greatest life through relinquishment, your greatest power through dependence and your greatest hope through surrender.

The specific details of my personal story, though significant to me, are less relevant to you. Each of us has a unique story; yet each of us has walked a similar journey to a place of brokenness. My prayer is that in drawing near to a place near God's altar, you will discover that God has reserved a table set for two, a place of intimate relationship with Him. This table is prepared with the clean linens of redemption and the lavish feast of His goodness, faithfulness and unfailing love to satisfy your soul day by day. May you discover over and over again how wide, long, deep and high the love of God is for you. May your heart become deeply rooted in this relationship that can never be removed, changed or dissolved. Anchored at the foot of the cross, may you find daily security and hope as you nourish your soul and nurture your children at "a place near [God's] altar."

FEAR OF THE FUTURE

Holding On to God When Life Is Falling Apart

It was the day after my twentieth wedding anniversary; my husband and I were separating. Not only had the music ended abruptly, but the dance floor had also fallen out from underneath me and I was in a free fall of sheer terror. Every emotional nerve ending screamed in anguish, yet I could hardly utter a word. How is it possible to be numb and feel pain at the same time? My stomach was a solid knot as my mind churned over the events of the last 48 hours. *I will never be okay again.*

"I would have despaired unless I had believed I would see the goodness of the LORD in the land of the living. Wait for the LORD; be strong and let your heart take courage; yes, wait for the LORD" (Psalm 27:13-14, *NASB*). Where did those words come from? My mind scrolled back 15 years; those words had been my mantra during my journey through infertility. Today, they reverberated in the back of my mind like a steady drumbeat as I mechanically drove to and from my afternoon appointment. I would have despaired . . . I would have despaired . . . yes . . . unless what? "Unless I had believed I would see the goodness of the Lord in the land of the living" . . . Lord, I cannot see ANYTHING good in my circumstances; they are more horrible than I could have ever imagined. I don't see a good outcome for my marriage, for me or for my three children. But Your Word says that YOU are good; so it must follow that if I walk with You, I will see Your goodness, even in the midst of this nightmare. Oh, God, help me; please show me glimpses of Your goodness today and every day. Show me how to put my hand, and my children's hands, into Your hand one day at a time.

That evening I began a dinnertime ritual with my children, identifying God's names and attributes, one by one, day by day. He was our Shepherd; He would take care of us, gather us in His arms and carry us. He was our Light, on a very dark path. He was our Comforter, reaching into the deepest corners of our fear and pain; He was our stable Rock when everything around us was crumbling. He was our Strength when we felt weak; He was our Helper in every situation. After dinner, we cuddled on the couch to read a few chapters of the allegory *Hinds Feet on High Places,* by Hannah Hurnard. We identified deeply with Much-Afraid on her unpredictable journey following the Shepherd of Love to the "high places." The comforting rhythm of this new routine created a small measure of order out of chaos. Remembering His name helped each of us put our hands in the hand of the only one who could offer us security in this violent storm.

A PLACE WHERE MY NAME IS REMEMBERED

I am who I am . . . The Lord . . . this is my name forever,
the name by which I am to be remembered from generation to generation.
EXODUS 3:14-15

The Lord is my rock, my fortress, and my deliverer;
my God is my rock, in whom I take refuge. He is my shield and
the horn of my salvation, my stronghold.
PSALM 18:2

The Lord is my shepherd, I shall not be in want.
PSALM 23:1

The Lord is my light and my salvation—whom shall I fear?
The Lord is the stronghold of my life—of whom shall I be afraid?
PSALM 27:1

God is our refuge and strength, an ever-present help in trouble. . . .
The Lord Almighty is with us; the God of Jacob is our fortress.
PSALM 46:1,11

I will set him securely on high, because he has known My name.
PSALM 91:14, *NASB*

FOR REFLECTION

Let Me remind you who I AM.
Each of My names comes with a promise that will give you comfort and hope.

I AM:

Your heavenly Father . . . who loves you perfectly.
Your Creator . . . the author of new beginnings.
Your Counselor . . . who will help you in every difficulty.
Your Provider . . . who will supply all your needs.
Your Savior . . . who forgives and accepts you.
Your Shelter . . . who hides you in the palm of My hand.
Your Redeemer . . . who salvages your life from the pit.
Your Healer . . . who binds up your wounds.
Your Comforter . . . who understands your hurts.
Your Strength . . . when you feel weak.
Your Peace . . . when life seems overwhelming.
The Faithful One . . . who will never leave you; I am with you always.
The God who hears . . . every prayer of your heart.
I AM the same yesterday, today, and tomorrow.

There are no surprises for God; He goes before you into every tomorrow. Today's promise of "I AM" is also tomorrow's promise of "I will be." The One you trust for eternity is the One who promises to hold you securely today. His perfect love for you was demonstrated on the cross: "perfect love drives out fear" (1 John 4:18). Day by day, release your fears to Him at the foot of the cross.

I said to the man who stood at the gate of the year, "Give me a light
that I may tread safely into the unknown." And he replied: "Go out into the
darkness and put your hand into the hand of God. That shall be to you
better than light and safer than a known way."
M. L. HASKINS

LIVING AT A PLACE NEAR HIS ALTAR

I AM reveals God as the One who is present and sufficient in every unpredictable situation today, and in every unknown tomorrow. Hannah Whitall Smith, a renowned nineteenth-century evangelist, called I AM the "unfinished name of God." What "unknowns" are you grappling with today?

Which of God's names or character traits do you need to rely on today?

INVITING YOUR CHILDREN TO HIS ALTAR

Relate God's name and His character to your child as you discuss situations or challenges your child is facing. What name of God does your child need to rely on today?

Pray with your child, claiming God's faithfulness to His own name and character. Point out specific answers to prayer.

As a family, create a "Book of Remembrance," journaling God's names and tangible ways you see His activity in your lives.

PRAYER NOTES AND PERSONAL REFLECTIONS

April 14, 2010
On my way to Seattle. I'm building a house for the kids and myself. I'm scared because I'm alone. I've always had Steve to rely on to make decisions together. Now we are going different directions in our lives. I know the kids are anxious to start school and enjoy their summer. I may call Joni to keep the boys for the summer. God is our shepard. He will protect my children from harm.

HEARTACHE

God Is with Us

"I just can't do this! It's not supposed to be this way!" I sputtered, as my emotional dam ruptured. For months, I had dreaded this—my first Christmas season without my husband, and my children's first without their dad. Now, the confusing mess of Christmas tree branches strewn across the floor was a visual picture of the emotional mess of our lives. My kids had wanted a real tree, but an artificial tree was all I could manage. *Would everything about this Christmas be artificial?* Beyond the daunting task of untangling and stringing the lights (which had always been my husband's task) loomed the challenge of overriding tangled emotions to produce some glimmer of holiday festivity for my children. In setting up the nativity scene, the ivory porcelain figures seemed too fragile and pristine to survive life in the real world. How would we ever get through the holidays?

How did Mary get through that first Christmas? Life hadn't turned out the way she had expected, either. Over the previous nine months, had she ever thought, *I just can't do this! It's not supposed to be this way* . . . Granted, the visitation of an angel had assured her that her undesirable circumstances were God-ordained and a sign of His favor, but even so, she had not been given a choice in the matter. Her only choice was in her response. What was it the angel said to her? "The Lord is with you . . . do not be afraid" (Luke 1:28,30). His announcement echoed Isaiah's prophecy: "The virgin will be with child and will give birth to a son, and will call him Immanuel" (Isaiah 7:14). Immanuel means "God with us." *Immanuel; you are not alone.* How tightly did Mary hold on to that promise?

Two thousand years ago, Jesus did not come to us as a fragile porcelain figure. He entered into the messiness of life in a dirty stable, as one who was vulnerable and needy, who felt pain, who cried. He grew as one who would become "despised and rejected by men, a man of sorrows, and familiar with suffering" (Isaiah 53:3). He lived as one who would be misunderstood, and He experienced loss, betrayal, abandonment and suffering beyond the scope of human imagination. Facing the cross, He ultimately said under great duress, "Yet not my will, but yours be done" (Luke 22:42). Love entered into and chose brokenness. "This is my body given for you" (Luke 22:19). *That* Jesus still chooses to share in my brokenness. In my own limited measure of suffering, He wraps me in His blanket of compassion, whispers "fear not" and invites me to taste of His grace.

At dinner the next evening, I noticed the nativity scene had been re-arranged, disregarding my efforts to display an artistically balanced panorama. Now the figurines were all clumped in the middle, crowding the manger. "Who messed with the nativity scene?" I asked critically.

My four-year-old proudly and matter-of-factly owned the deed. "I did! They were too far away from baby Jesus. They needed to be closer so they could see him!" Out of the mouths of babes! She "got" what I had missed.

I kept her rearrangement; it was a daily reminder to position myself to see Jesus in the center of Christmas and in the center of our lives. Everything had changed for us this Christmas, except the main thing: Immanuel, God with us. We were not alone. God condescended to meet us in the broken places of our lives. As I celebrated the promise of His name, genuine joy invaded each day. "Joy to the world; the Lord has come!"

A PLACE WHERE MY NAME IS REMEMBERED

*The virgin will be with child and will give birth to a son,
and will call him Immanuel.*
ISAIAH 7:14

So do not fear, for I am with you; do not be dismayed, for I am your God. I will strengthen you and help you. I will uphold you with my righteous right hand.
ISAIAH 41:10

*When you pass through the waters, I will be with you; and when you pass
through the rivers, they will not sweep over you . . . for I am the Lord, your God,
the Holy One of Israel, your Savior.*

ISAIAH 43:2-3

The Lord is close to the brokenhearted and saves those who are crushed in spirit.

PSALM 34:18

*His name will be called Wonderful Counselor, Mighty God,
Everlasting Father, Prince of Peace.*

ISAIAH 9:6, *NASB*

*I will ask the Father, and he will give you another Counselor who will be with you
forever . . . for he lives with you, and will be in you. I will not leave you as orphans; I will come to you.*

JOHN 14:16-18

FOR REFLECTION

God drew near to us in Jesus so that we could draw near to Him
through Jesus. He was rejected so that we could be accepted; broken
so that we could be made whole; suffered death on the cross so that
we could receive the gift of eternal life. At the foot of the cross, you are
invited to unwrap the amazing gift of a love relationship with God
through Jesus Christ, Immanuel, "God with us."

LIVING AT A PLACE NEAR HIS ALTAR

What does the name Immanuel, "God with us," mean to you in today's
bundle of circumstances?

How can you rely on Him today as your Wonderful Counselor, Mighty
God, Everlasting Father, Prince of Peace?

What "blocks your view" of Jesus? How can you reposition yourself
today to keep Him in view?

INVITING YOUR CHILDREN TO HIS ALTAR

Ask your children to set a place at the dinner table for Jesus as your "guest of honor." Let them select one of the names of God for the place card; ask them why that particular name is meaningful.

Explain to your children how to receive the gift of life offered through Jesus by His death on the cross. Do not pressure them to respond; trust His love to draw them in time.

Each morning, identify the challenges your children are facing that day; focus on God's name and pray His blessing on them as the day begins.

The LORD bless you and keep you; the LORD make his face shine upon you and be gracious to you; the LORD turn his face toward you and give you peace.
NUMBERS 6:24-26

PRAYER NOTES AND PERSONAL REFLECTIONS

8 Apr 2014

Our first xmas picture without Steve was difficult. Anna was throwing a fit because she did not want to wear matching dresses with her little sister Natalie. The boys did not want to dress up but could see how anxious I was. They were easy going.
Recently we spend xmas with Steve. It took time to forgive and heal. He is there for the kids. I know we are not meant to be. But we can be there for our kids.

FORGETFULNESS

When We Need Help Remembering His Name

"Is your name 'Forgetful' today?" I teased, gently jogging my preschool daughter's memory. Bethany Joy's blank stare morphed into a studied frown, followed by an "aha!" moment of recollection.

Short attention spans give children a reasonable excuse when they forget. However, forgetfulness continues to plague me in midlife, exacerbated by stress and fatigue. As a single mom, I often feel like the absent-minded professor. Remembering names is particularly difficult for me. When our family relocated, I would frequently find myself in the midst of friendly conversations wondering, *Who is this? What is her name?* Had we met at one of my children's schools or at a church we had visited? With embarrassment, I apologized as I asked the person's name again. *How do you build a relationship with someone if you don't know or can't remember his or her name?*

Remembering someone's name honors him or her with significance. Our name is the most basic label of our identity; we are known by our name. Surnames, family names, nicknames and names of endearment identify us personally and relationally. Names also have powerful associations. Widows often cherish their deceased partner's name; whereas, divorcées are often eager to shed their married name. In the Bible, names often carried prophetic weight about an individual's character (Jacob, the "Deceiver") or mission (Jesus, the "Savior").

Our loving God knows and remembers each of us by name. He wants to be known by us, so He gave us His names: Jehovah-jireh (the God who Provides); Jehovah-rapha (the God who Heals); El Shaddai (God Almighty); El Roi (the God who sees me). But He knows we are forgetful; we need our memory jogged. In the Old Testament, He established altars as places for His people to remember His name, His character, their identity as His chosen people and His activity among them. When they honored His name, He promised to come to them and bless them (see Exodus 20:24). The altar was a place of sacrifice and a place of meeting with God—foreshadowing the cross where the Lamb of God offered the ultimate sacrifice to establish a permanent relationship with those He loves.

A Roman soldier who witnessed the crucifixion realized the Truth and exclaimed, "Surely this man was the Son of God" (Mark 15:39). His quiet confession and proclamation at the foot of the cross has been echoing for generations. The altar of the cross is the place where His name has been remembered and celebrated for 2,000 years. All around the world, communion tables engraved with the words, "This do in remembrance of Me," invite us to the foot of the cross to remember His name, bringing into focus who He is, who we are and the amazing love relationship He initiated and pursues with us.

Sadly, forgetfulness seems to be part of our human condition. We can easily get caught up in the moment, find ourselves derailed by the current "crisis," or see things from a myopically self-centered perspective. Like little children, we need help remembering. Worshiping God for who He is; praise and thanksgiving for what He has done; praying, even when we don't feel like it; reading and reflecting on Scripture; celebrating communion; cultivating relationships with others who love Jesus—these holy habits are the "strings" we tie around our fingers, helping us remember the One whose love we dare not forget.

Is your name "Forgetful" today?

A PLACE OF REMEMBERING HIS NAME

Build my altar wherever I cause my name to be remembered,
and I will come to you and bless you.
EXODUS 20:24, *NLT*

I will cause Your name to be remembered in all generations; therefore the peoples
will give You thanks forever and ever.
PSALM 45:17, *NASB*

*I will exalt you, my God and King, and praise your name forever
and ever. . . . Let each generation tell its children of your
mighty acts; let them proclaim your power.*
PSALM 145:1,4, *NLT*

*And being found in appearance as a man, he humbled himself and
became obedient to death—even death on a cross! Therefore God
exalted him to the highest place and gave him the name that is above
every name, that at the name of Jesus every knee should bow, in heaven
and on earth and under the earth, and every tongue confess that
Jesus Christ is Lord, to the glory of God the Father.*
PHILIPPIANS 2:8-11

FOR REFLECTION

The names of God reveal His essence—correcting our distortions,
bringing Him more accurately into focus and inviting us to love, worship and rely on Him. Meditate on the following list of God's names:

Elohim: "Creator, Mighty and Strong" (Genesis 1:1)
El Roi: "The God Who Sees" (Genesis 16:13)
Jehovah-jireh: "The Lord Will Provide" (Genesis 22:14)
El Shaddai: "God Almighty" (Genesis 49:24)
Jehovah-rapha: "The Lord Who Heals" (Exodus 15:26)
Jehovah-shalom: "The Lord Our Peace" (Judges 6:23-24)
Jehovah-raah: "The Lord Our Shepherd" (Psalm 23:1)
Jehovah-tsidkenu: "The Lord Our Righteousness"
    (2 Corinthians 5:21)

LIVING AT A PLACE NEAR HIS ALTAR

When are you prone to forget God's name?

What names of God invite you to rely on Him this week in your particular set of circumstances?

What "strings" can you "tie on your fingers" to help you remember His name and bring Him clearly into focus?

INVITING YOUR CHILDREN TO HIS ALTAR

As a family, have fun looking up the meanings of each child's name(s). Identify the ways your children live out the meaning of their names.

Using blank three-by-five-inch cards, create a "lotto" game with your children, using a list of the Hebrew names of God and their English equivalent (available on the Internet). Play the game by finding the matching pairs of Hebrew/English names. See who can remember a Bible story illustrating how God lived up to His name.

The earliest altars in the Old Testament were piles of rocks marking when God revealed Himself in a personal way at a certain time or place. Collect some small rocks, and invite each family member to help build a small "family altar" to recall specific ways God has answered prayer, intervened in circumstances or revealed truth about Himself to them.

PRAYER NOTES AND PERSONAL REFLECTIONS

9 Apr 2014

Thank you Lord for a beautiful sunny day. We are at Ocean Shores for Spring Break. I had a difficult time going to mass with Steve last Sunday. I want to go with just the kids and me. I feel like JBUM is our church not his for me to share. Please forgive me. I need to be a better person.

SELF-WORTH

Finding Your Intrinsic Value in God's Unconditional Love

Relationships and roles carry tremendous defining power, raising us to a sense of significance or reducing us in shame. Shortly after her divorce, my friend Cheryl confided, "I feel like I'm walking around with a big scarlet *D* on my chest." She felt like a "second-class Christian" in her church when she was asked to step down from a ministry role. Her Sunday School class was full of awkward moments, accentuating her sense of incompleteness without a spouse; can a single sign up for a Dinner-for-8 group, which is neatly designed for four couples? Cheryl had always been a hands-on involved mom. Now, the demands of her new job required her to forfeit her position as room mother and Girl Scout leader, and her role as a mom felt marginalized by shared custody. Reluctantly shedding layers of relationships and roles as a wife, leader, friend and super-mom, *D* meant divorced, defrocked, disenfranchised, diminished, devalued. Cheryl had always defined herself in terms of these relationships and roles; who was she now?

Sadly, most of us define ourselves and find our identity—our sense of worth-*full*-ness—in our relationships or roles. We usually don't realize it until that source of identity is stripped away, leaving a sense of worth-*less*-ness. All too easily, single moms scramble to recover their sense of value and significance through remarriage, chasing accolades at work or catering to their children's whims.

In the beginning, our lives are weighed on a very different scale. Do you remember the wonder-filled moments of holding your newborn baby swaddled in your arms? Your baby's worth was rooted solely in the fact that this was *your* baby. Your child was precious apart from any significant accomplishment (beyond filling a diaper!) and without proving himself or herself through any achievement (beyond burping!). You would do *anything* for the life of your child. This is but a small glimpse of how your heavenly Father loves and values you, His precious one!

Your intrinsic value is bound up in God's unconditional love for you. Because He created you for Himself, you are of infinite worth to Him. He intricately designed every part of your being; you are His unique handiwork, created by Him and for Him and He delights in you! Your worth to God is not based on your performance or achievements; the Bible says that all our good works are like "filthy rags" to Him. In fact, our sin makes us *unworthy* to come to God because He is holy. But God's desire for an intimate relationship with you compelled Him to bridge the separation created by sin, taking the penalty of death upon Himself and giving you His righteousness. The One who knew you before the foundation of the world demonstrated His extravagant love by giving the life of His own Son, for your sake. This is astonishing grace: the worthy One died to make you worthy; the holy One died to make you holy!

At the foot of the cross, what can be added to His ultimate statement of your worth? When validation from other sources is lacking (as it most often will be), the cup of your worth-*full*-ness remains full to the brim, full of the significance and value given you by God in Jesus Christ. When other relationships and roles are stripped away, the cross of Christ remains fixed in time. It is a reminder of the one essential relationship that can never be altered or removed, the one defining relationship that declares your ultimate worth in Christ Jesus.

A PLACE OF IDENTITY

For the Lord your God is living among you. He is a mighty savior.
He will take delight in you with gladness. With his love, he will calm all your fears.
He will rejoice over you with joyful songs.
ZEPHANIAH 3:17, *NLT*

Are not two sparrows sold for a penny? Yet not one of them will fall to the ground
apart from the will of your Father. And even the very hairs of your head are all
numbered. So don't be afraid; you are worth more than many sparrows.
MATTHEW 10:29-31

Now, most people would not be willing to die for an upright person, though someone might perhaps be willing to die for a person who is especially good. But God showed his great love for us by sending Christ to die for us while we were still sinners. And since we have been made right in God's sight by the blood of Christ, he will certainly save us from God's condemnation.

ROMANS 5:7-10, *NLT*

God saved you by his grace when you believed. And you can't take credit for this; it is a gift from God. Salvation is not a reward for the good things we have done, so none of us can boast about it.

EPHESIANS 2:8-9, *NLT*

For in Christ lives all the fullness of God in a human body. So you also are complete through your union with Christ, who is the head over every ruler and authority.

COLOSSIANS 2:9-10, *NLT*

FOR REFLECTION

Jesus frequently asked His disciples, "Who do you say I am?" It is a question He still asks today. This is not just a theology quiz; the answer has significant ramifications for our own identity as well. If Jesus were just a good teacher or a wise man, then His words would be merely added to the disputable voices of many others throughout time. However, pronouncements of our worth from the King of kings and Lord of lords carry incomparable weight!

LIVING AT A PLACE NEAR HIS ALTAR

What relationships or roles have seductively given you a sense of your worth?

As a single mom, where do you tend to look for validation of your worth?

How does your perspective change at the foot of the cross, when you consider the price Jesus willingly paid to bring you to God?

INVITING YOUR CHILDREN TO HIS ALTAR

Wrap your children in God's love by saying "I love you" *often*, not just when they are "good," but especially when they have "messed up."

Read Psalm 139 with your children. Remind them that they are one-of-a-kind precious gifts from God. Identify your child's unique strengths, talents and positive character traits, *apart from* performance-related affirmations.

Tell your children how you felt about them that first time you held them in your arms. Relate what you love about being their mom, identifying the ways they bring joy to your life.

PRAYER NOTES AND PERSONAL REFLECTIONS

When I held Micael in my arms I was overjoyed with love! I wanted to share him with everyone. He is the first grandson on both sides of the family.

Anna came out crying. I was surprise. Her Dad fainted because we almost lost Micael at birth. Anna is strong. I nursed her for two years because I thought she was our last baby.

Patrick was sick when he came out. I was afraid for him. I was mobilized to Ft. Bliss, TX when he was ten months old.

Natalie is the baby. We could not hear her heart beat for six weeks so I prayed for her a lot.

SHAME

*God Removes Our Shame and Gives Us
a New Identity in Christ*

"Sticks and stones may break my bones but names will never hurt me!"
Whoever coined that little ditty was *so wrong*. Names label us, for good
or for bad. Hurtful names assigned by foolish children have the power
to haunt us into adulthood. Affirming labels can be equally powerful,
informing our choices and fueling behaviors to maintain them. People
often expend tremendous energy trying to outlive a negative name or
live up to a positive name. From the day we are born, others give us
names, and these names can become our source of identity. They can
be either crippling or empowering.

"Whenever I'm around her, my name is 'Loser'." My friend wore this
name for 20 years whenever she was in the presence of her ex-husband's
second wife, with whom he had had an affair. That powerful name held
my friend captive, robbing her of many opportunities to enjoy times
with her children and grandchildren at family gatherings. Sadly, it is a
name she gave herself, and it hung like a millstone around her neck.

Listening to the stories of other single moms, I've heard their un-
spoken names: Failure; Rejected; Defective; Incomplete; Alone; Insignificant; Invisible; Victim. Whether labeled by others or by
themselves, these aliases reflect what they believe about themselves.
They alternately descend to these labels in resignation or exhaust
themselves trying to transcend them. Either way, these women are in
bondage to the same hidden identity: Shame.

Shame has been lurking inside of us since the Garden of Eden; it
is the first emotion recorded after Adam and Eve sinned. Our outward
experiences tend to confirm what we already know about ourselves on
some level: we are "broken" people who fall short of God's standard.

Like Adam and Eve, shame sends us into hiding—from others, from God, from ourselves. Shame hides in unexpected places: perfectionism, overachievement, underachievement, status, addictions. Jesus came to bring us out of hiding, to live in the light of His grace.

Jesus knew many women with that same identity of Shame. One woman, labeled "unclean" for 12 years, due to her physical malady, fearfully reached through the press of the crowd to touch Jesus' robe, believing He could heal her. In response to her faith, He gave her a new name of acceptance, "Daughter," and the blessing of emotional peace and physical healing (see Mark 5:24-34). Another woman was called "adulteress" by her religious accusers (see John 8:1-11). Jesus silenced them, refused to condemn her and invited her to a new way of living. To a minority woman who had five previous husbands and a current illicit relationship, Jesus offered "living water"—quenching her thirst for significance and security and cleansing her from the inside out. Transformed by His unconditional love, her story of shame became a joyful proclamation of hope (see John 4:1-42). In yet another account, Jesus gave a "woman of ill-repute" a new reputation, making an example of her humble worship provoked by brokenness and love. Through Jesus, she found significance and the blessing of forgiveness and peace (see John 7:36-50). Jesus offered each of these women a new identity as recipients of His unconditional love, removing their shrouds of shame, and clothing them in His righteousness.

Jesus knows your story and loves you completely. The One who is the Name above all names invites you to discard all your shaming aliases at the foot of His cross, see yourself as His beloved and find your identity in the grace of His unconditional love. He longs to fill you with His Spirit to empower you to live as a "saint"—one "set apart" for His purposes.

What is your name?

A PLACE OF IDENTITY

*But now, this is what the Lord says—he who created you, O Jacob,
he who formed you, O Israel: "Fear not, for I have redeemed you; I have
summoned you by name; you are mine."*
ISAIAH 43:1

*Fear not; you will no longer live in shame. Don't be afraid; there is no more
disgrace for you. You will no longer remember the shame of your
youth and the sorrows of widowhood. For your Creator will be your husband;
the LORD of Heaven's Armies is his name! He is your Redeemer,
the Holy One of Israel, the God of all the earth.*
ISAIAH 54:4-5, *NLT*

*For everyone has sinned; we all fall short of God's glorious standard. Yet God,
with undeserved kindness, declares that we are righteous. He did this through
Christ Jesus when he freed us from the penalty for our sins. For God presented
Jesus as the sacrifice for sin. People are made right with God when they
believe that Jesus sacrificed his life, shedding his blood.*
ROMANS 3:23-25, *NLT*

*Even before he made the world, God loved us and chose us in
Christ to be holy and without fault in his eyes.*
EPHESIANS 1:4, *NLT*

*All who are victorious will be clothed in white. I will never erase
their names from the Book of Life, but I will announce before
my Father and his angels that they are mine.*
REVELATION 3:5, *NLT*

FOR REFLECTION

Jesus was shamed by others so that you could be freed from shame.
Jesus experienced disgrace so that you could experience His grace.
Jesus became a victim in death to give you victory in life.
Jesus emptied Himself to give you fullness in Him.
Jesus gave His life for you so that you could live your life for Him.

LIVING AT A PLACE NEAR HIS ALTAR

What shaming aliases have labeled you? Where do you "hide" from
your shame?

Holding on to negative labels can enable you to avoid taking responsibility for your present choices and circumstances. How are you hindered by negative labels?

How different would your choices look if you lived in the truth of your identity as God's "precious child," His "beloved" and as an "empowered saint"?

INVITING YOUR CHILDREN TO THE ALTAR

What names have labeled your children? Avoid inadvertently projecting shame on your children through comparison, sarcasm, or critical perfectionism.

When disciplining your children, be careful to identify their inappropriate behaviors ("Your tone of voice is disrespectful") rather than label their person ("You are a disrespectful child").

Children of divorce often feel shamed if their family is called a "broken family." Explain that all families are broken in one way or another, due to sin; divorce unmasks that brokenness. Explain that Jesus died on the cross to heal the ways our lives have been broken by sin.

PRAYER NOTES AND PERSONAL REFLECTIONS

_____

_____

_____

_____

_____

_____

_____

_____

_____

REDEFINING LIFE

Finding Your Life in Christ

As I pulled my car slowly into my garage, I noticed the doorframe around the garage's side door had pulled away from the wall, exposing long nails. "Huh, I wonder when that happened?" I mused out loud. Inside, I groaned, *One more thing to get fixed.*

Depositing my belongings in the kitchen, I noticed a small red satin jewelry pouch on the table. "Grace, what have you been into today?" I queried the cat.

My daughter Emily followed me into our family room. "Mom, where's my laptop?" she asked. We both stared at the vacant desktop. Suddenly, my brain connected the dots from the garage door to the kitchen table to the empty desktop. Our home had been burglarized!

"Wait here, Emily; let me look around." Phew! My grandmother's flatware was still in the silver chest in the dining room. But when I walked into my bedroom, it was a mess! Dresser drawers were hanging out, small jewelry boxes were strewn across the dresser top and my velvet earring case was missing. A desk drawer was also ajar, with banking papers and boxes of checks in disarray. My closet had also been ransacked. I quickly dialed 9-1-1.

While waiting for the police, I took inventory of what was missing—and more noticeably, what was NOT missing. A glass box of costume jewelry had been emptied, but the opened dresser drawers still held my jewelry trays, including a few gemstone rings and 14K gold necklaces that were irreplaceable because of their sentimental value. Although someone had pilfered through my boxes of checks, none were missing. My most important documents were in a safety deposit box at the bank. Thankfully, my laptop had been with me at work;

none of our other electronics were taken. Our most valuable items had been left behind! Instead of being upset about what was lost, I felt relieved and grateful for what remained.

When my husband and I separated, I felt like our family had been robbed—robbed of invaluable and irreplaceable security, trust, love and hope. Everything was in shambles; the drawers of my life hung open, exposing painful memories, present confusion and fear of the future. The reality was both jarring and numbing. Every day, many times a day, I would think, *I can't believe this is my life!*

One day, Paul's words in Colossians stopped me in my tracks. "Set your mind on things above, not on earthly things. For you died, and your life is now hidden with Christ in God. When *Christ, who is your life,* appears, then you also will appear with him in glory" (Colossians 3:2-4, emphasis mine). The words jumped off the page. Paul was stating that *Christ—Christ Himself* was my "life." All my painful circumstances were just that—circumstances surrounding my life. But my true life was Christ Himself, and that core remained untouched. No one could steal the love, trust, security or hope I had in my relationship with Christ! All of that remained securely sealed in the safety deposit box of my soul. Instead of looking at my unbelievable set of circumstances, I began focusing on the unbelievable richness of my relationship with God, the precious promises that were mine in Christ and the invaluable blessing of His presence and power in my life. Delighting in those life-changing realities gave new, positive meaning to my mantra: *I can't believe this—Christ—is my life!*

Satan has been "robbing" us since the beginning of time—stealing our joy, killing our hope, destroying our relationships with God and others. But on the altar of the cross, Jesus' death interrupted Satan's work. Through God's gift of salvation, we have been given a new inner life that is secure and impenetrable, sealed by the power of the Holy Spirit. The enemy of our souls may still try to wreak havoc in our lives, at great cost to us and others, but he can *never* walk off with our true life, our life that is hidden with Christ in God. Satan may delight in disrupting our circumstances and throwing our lives in disarray, but God is faithful to restore what has been lost in unusual and surprising ways.

A PLACE OF IDENTITY

Don't store up treasures here on earth, where moths eat them and rust destroys them, and where thieves break in and steal. Store your treasures in heaven, where moths and rust cannot destroy, and thieves do not break in and steal. Wherever your treasure is, there the desires of your heart will also be.
MATTHEW 6:19-21, *NLT*

The thief comes only to steal and kill and destroy; I have come that they may have life, and have it to the full.
JOHN 10:10

He has identified us as his own by placing the Holy Spirit in our hearts as the first installment that guarantees everything he has promised us.
2 CORINTHIANS 1:22, *NLT*

I once thought these things were valuable, but now I consider them worthless because of what Christ has done. Yes, everything else is worthless when compared with the infinite value of knowing Christ Jesus my Lord. For his sake I have discarded everything else, counting it all as garbage, so that I could gain Christ.
PHILIPPIANS 3:7-8, *NLT*

Think about the things of heaven, not the things of earth. For you died to this life, and your real life is hidden with Christ in God. And when Christ, who is your life, is revealed to the whole world, you will share in all his glory.
COLOSSIANS 3:2-4, *NLT*

FOR REFLECTION

Whatever you treasure shapes your heart, your attitudes and your actions.

LIVING AT A PLACE NEAR HIS ALTAR

How has your identity been defined by what you "treasure"?

What have you "lost" that you hope Christ will restore?

What has Christ given you that can never be lost? *Mom + DAD*
Michel, Anna, Patrick, Natalie,

INVITING YOUR CHILDREN TO HIS ALTAR

Discuss where your kids "find life." Do they find it in activities, in sports, in social status?

Discuss the "life" that is promised through advertisements. How long does that life last?

As a family, read Ephesians 1, making a list of the permanent blessings God has given you in Christ. Tuck the list in an envelope; write the name "Jesus Christ" on the outside, and seal the envelope. Explain that when your children receive God's gift of salvation, they are "hidden" in Jesus Christ and "sealed" by the Holy Spirit, securing every eternal blessing.

PRAYER NOTES AND PERSONAL REFLECTIONS

IDENTITY

Longing for Belonging

"Who do you belong to, honey?" a concerned woman asked my bewildered daughter amid a sea of parents after her preschool Christmas pageant. Robin anxiously looked about; when her eyes finally locked with mine, she smiled broadly and pointed. My eyes had been on her the whole time, but from her vantage point, I had been obscured from view. She ran to hug me and relaxed in my embrace. With her small fingers wrapped around mine, the swarming crowd no longer mattered.

From the time we are small, we are busy identifying who we belong to: our parents; our siblings; playground playmates; middle-school cliques; athletic teams; college sororities; a spouse. Belonging to someone offers a sense of security; who we belong to can easily become an extension of our identity.

Newly divorced, Cindy anxiously confessed, "I don't want to be alone!" She was successful in business, was financially secure, physically attractive and socially savvy. However, her fear of being "unattached" and her desperate need to belong to someone propelled her into a whirlwind romance and rebound marriage long before she sorted out the demise of her first marriage.

Anne, envying the proximity of my extended family, often lamented, "But I don't have any family here!" despite her circle of supportive friendships. Reading between the lines, I knew she was longing for belonging. As a single mom, *Who do you belong to, honey?*

The sense of belonging that is the by-product of marriage and family relationships reflects the way we are hard-wired by God for relational security—precious, enduring relationships that offer the emotional safety of being loved no matter what. When those relationships are tragically severed, there is an indescribable rupture deep within the soul.

However, at the very deepest levels, our longing for belonging was never intended to be satisfied completely in other people. Because we are made in the image of God, we have been "created by him and for him" (Colossians 1:16). This is a deep, intimate relationship the Bible alternately likens to the husband–wife and parent–child relationships of belonging.

The Bible is the unfolding story of God's overtures to establish this relationship of belonging with us. From the time of Noah, to Abraham, to Moses, to Jesus Christ, the Bible reveals a passionate, pursuing, covenant-making God wooing His "bride" and pledging His unconditional love and faithfulness. Even when Israel rebelled, God's love was relentless: " 'But then I will win her back once again. I will lead her into the desert and speak tenderly to her there. . . . When that day comes,' says the LORD, 'you will call me "my husband" instead of "my master." . . . I will make you my wife forever, showing you righteousness and justice, unfailing love and compassion. I will be faithful to you and make you mine, and you will finally know me as the LORD' " (Hosea 2:14,16,19-20, *NLT*).

In the Old Testament, altars were places where God's covenant promises were ratified, remembered and reaffirmed by His people whom He affectionately called His "treasured possession" (Deuteronomy 7:6). Ultimately, He betrothed Himself to us on the altar of the cross—a covenant relationship of ultimate security sealed forever with the blood of Jesus. *This is my body, broken for you; this the new covenant of my blood, shed for you.* Love spanned the distance from heaven to the cross so that we might belong to Him as His beloved, as His bride.

At best, earthly relationships remain imperfect and impermanent; but in this intimate relationship with God through Jesus Christ, we are fully known, completely accepted and faithfully loved and cherished—in the present and for the long haul through eternity! By God's design, our deepest longings for belonging are fully satisfied in Him alone.

A PLACE OF BELONGING

For your Maker is your husband—the Lord Almighty is his name—the Holy One
of Israel is your Redeemer; he is called the God of all the earth.
ISAIAH 54:5

As a bridegroom rejoices over his bride, so will your God rejoice over you.
ISAIAH 62:5

*They will be my people, and I will be their God. I will give them
singleness of heart and action, so that they will always fear me for their
own good and the good of their children after them.*
JEREMIAH 32:38-39

*Don't you realize that your body is the temple of the Holy Spirit,
who lives in you and was given to you by God? You do not belong
to yourself, for God bought you with a high price.*
1 CORINTHIANS 6:19-20, *NLT*

FOR REFLECTION

Just as my preschooler had difficulty finding me in the press of the
crowd, sometimes our view of God is obstructed by people or circumstances. But He has His eye on you and longs for you to put your hand
in His and press into the embrace of His love. Daily intimate fellowship with God will anchor you in the One who knows and satisfies
the deepest longings of your soul. Lay your longing for belonging at
the foot of the cross, where He paid the ultimate price for you to belong to Him.

LIVING AT A PLACE NEAR HIS ALTAR

What temptations accompany your desires for relational security?

What distractions and other affections get in the way of finding your
desires satisfied in Jesus?

When you are feeling "empty," allow the Lord to fill your "emotional
tank" as you express your worship and love through praise. Cultivate
a habit of praise by keeping a worship CD handy in the car, in the
kitchen or even in your computer!

INVITING YOUR CHILDREN TO HIS ALTAR

Make family times a nonnegotiable priority: plan regular family meal times and biweekly "family activity time" to play games, read together, or go on a special outing.

Draw a picture of your family tree to help your children see where they "fit" in their extended family. Consider creating a family circular letter or a family blog for your extended family to stay connected through regular updates.

Share God's wonderful plan with your children: "God decided in advance to adopt us into his own family by bringing us to himself through Jesus Christ. This is what he wanted to do, and it gave him great pleasure" (Ephesians 1:5, *NLT*). Explain how your children can belong to God's family (see John 1:12-13); identify the many metaphors of belonging that Jesus used to describe our relationship with Him: Father–son (see Luke 15); shepherd–sheep (see John 10); vine–branches (see John 15).

PRAYER NOTES AND PERSONAL REFLECTIONS

_____

_____

_____

_____

_____

_____

_____

_____

_____

_____

_____

_____

_____

ACCEPTANCE

God Knows Me and Loves Me as I Am

Under the basement staircase of our old house, I created a "dress-up closet" for the girls. Old bridesmaid dresses and play makeup transformed my daughter Emily and her cousin Anna into princesses and beauty queens. Donning assorted shoes and hats, the preschoolers stepped into the make-believe world of their imagination. *They could be whoever they wanted to be!* They were especially thrilled if I let them wear their costumes out in public. The magic might even work "out there," fooling others to believe they were real princesses!

But in the real world, little girls discover quickly that who they are or who they want to be is often not readily accepted by others. As they grow older, the game of "pretend" changes. Incrementally burying the real self in the tomb of the soul, they learn to play to their audience—first to their parents, then to their peers—becoming whoever *others* want them to be! Eventually, the "real self" is buried alive.

Over and over, my female clients relate the same story. They are adults now but still wearing masks and costumes—to work, to church, to their kids' school events. Some masks project having-it-all-together, self-sufficiency or indifference. Some wear costumes of Superwoman, perfectionism or the armor of invulnerability. However, now there are cracks in the masks, and the costumes are becoming threadbare. Vulnerabilities have become exposed as the façade of their marriages have crumbled. "Pretending" no longer works. Their trail of pain leads us inward, where we begin unwrapping and resuscitating this mummified "real self" that believed a lie. The lie has many versions, but the bottom line is the same: *If people really knew me, they wouldn't love me.* For many single moms, the wounds of failed relationships reinforce this lie. The "real self" longs for unconditional acceptance.

Jesus met a woman who believed this lie and knew this longing. She had tried to fix the ache inside with a string of husbands. She paid a price along the way as each man took a piece of her soul but left her behind, their wounds of rejection reinforcing the lie. Now she had another intimate partner. (Since he might leave, too, why even bother getting married?) Imagine her surprise when Jesus asked for water in the heat of the day—a Jew condescending to make a request of a Samaritan, yet with respect. A man asking her to satisfy his thirst, but wanting only water! Jesus, knowing that she was the one whose soul was truly parched, offered to slake *her* thirst permanently—just for the asking. Was it possible to have her thirst truly satisfied—forever? Can Someone be trusted who offers you something for nothing, and offers it for keeps?

Knowing the questions of her heart, Jesus began to tell her the truth—about herself, about God and about Himself. Looking past her nationality, past her gender and past her past, He offered her acceptance, disempowered the lie that had enslaved her and invited her to a new way of living. No longer bound by the fear of rejection, she eagerly invited others to taste the life-giving water Jesus offered—the freedom of unconditional love and acceptance. "He knew all about the things I did. He knows me inside and out!" (John 4:39, *THE MESSAGE*).

I've learned that certain people or situations temporarily draw me back to the power of the lie, prompting me to slip on a protective mask. But the lie only has power when I choose to believe it. Instead, Jesus empowers me with this truth: by God's grace, my real self is lovable and acceptable. I can strip off my smothering masks and ill-fitting costumes at the foot of the cross and exchange them for His robe of righteousness. Knowing us completely, and loving us unconditionally, Jesus paid for our sin and embraces us as His beloved. He knows us inside out, loves us inside out and offers us His life-giving Spirit of love flowing from the inside out. In new freedom, we can be—and become—the women *He* wants us to be!

A PLACE OF IDENTITY

For you created my inmost being; you knit me together in my mother's womb. I praise you because I am fearfully and wonderfully made; your works are wonderful, I know that full well.
PSALM 139:13-14

Do not be afraid; you will not suffer shame. Do not fear disgrace; you will not be humiliated. You will forget the shame of your youth and remember no more the reproach of your widowhood.
ISAIAH 54:4

The LORD appeared to us in the past, saying: "I have loved you with an everlasting love; I have drawn you with loving-kindness."
JEREMIAH 31:3

For God presented Jesus as the sacrifice for sin. People are made right with God when they believe that Jesus sacrificed his life, shedding his blood. . . . God did this to demonstrate his righteousness, for he himself is fair and just, and he declares sinners to be right in his sight when they believe in Jesus. Can we boast, then, that we have done anything to be accepted by God? No, because our acquittal is not based on obeying the law. It is based on faith.
ROMANS 3:25-27, NLT

There is no fear in love. But perfect love drives out fear, because fear has to do with punishment. The one who fears is not made perfect in love.
1 JOHN 4:18

FOR REFLECTION

It is safe to come out of hiding; God knows the real you intimately and loves the real you completely. Nothing you do can make Him love you more, and nothing you do can make Him love you less.

LIVING AT A PLACE NEAR HIS ALTAR

What "masks" or "costumes" do you wear?

What situations trigger you to believe "the lie"?

What is the truth that Jesus would say about you?

INVITING YOUR CHILDREN TO HIS ALTAR

Using paper plates, ask your children to create masks of the person they would like to be. What character traits or qualities does that person have?

Find out what your child likes and dislikes about himself/herself. Identify the positive qualities God has given your child, and affirm ways those traits can be a blessing to others.

Using a washable glass-marking pen, create a "picture frame" on your child's bathroom (or handheld) mirror. Write your child's character traits around the edge of the mirror; across the top, write, "God loves me."

PRAYER NOTES AND PERSONAL REFLECTIONS

_____
_____
_____
_____
_____
_____
_____
_____
_____
_____
_____
_____
_____

ISOLATION

Finding Connection and Purpose in the Body of Christ

Church-shopping after our cross-country relocation was an arduous drill. Were it not for the purpose of establishing some sense of stability, security and "sameness" of routine for my children, I might have easily signed off on the miserable ordeal. Visiting an adult Sunday School class, *alone*, was particularly awkward. Walking in by myself, I felt invisible as others enjoyed chatty conversations. At one church, I decided to embrace my new status by visiting an "Older Single Adults" class. After a bit of detective work, I found an obscure room tucked in a remote corner of the building and discovered a small band of random singles seated around a table. At least they were welcoming; my presence increased their numbers by a significant percentage! Nevertheless, after several weeks in that group, the only obvious common denominator I could detect was their "single" status, reminding me of the odd socks floating around my sock drawer. I felt myself suffocating, both spiritually and socially; *I will DIE if I have to stay in this group to have a place of belonging in this church!*

That day, I resolved to refuse to define myself or my place in the Body of Christ by my marital status. In Christ, we have a place of belonging that supersedes cultural and social distinctions. The apostle Paul flat-out rejected any preoccupation with such categories, stressing instead the unity we have through our common bond in Christ. Jesus made us brothers and sisters to Himself and to one another. Paul likened our place of belonging in the church to the human body; in Christ, we belong to one another because we belong to the Head, who is Christ, and are filled with His indwelling Holy Spirit. Paul elevated the significance and importance of each part for the overall function of the body. Our niche and function in the Body of Christ is determined by the gifting of the Spirit—not by marital status, social status, financial status or any other superficial distinction. *Follow your gifts; they will lead you into your "place" in the Body.* Someone with a passion for music and the gift of encouragement will likely find a place of belonging in the worship ministry; one with a heart for missions and the gift of serving may find common bonds of friendship and fellowship on a missions committee or outreach team.

All too easily, single moms who feel uncomfortable in the church abdicate their place in the Body of Christ, becoming passive pew warmers or opting for the "solo spirituality" popularized in the Western world. Work-weary weekend fatigue offers an easy excuse to isolate but discounts God's design and purposes. Can my foot decide to stay in bed for the day while the rest of my body accomplishes God's work in the world? Can my arm arbitrarily separate itself from my torso without a negative impact both on that limb and the rest of my body? The exercise of our gifts is vital for our own spiritual health as well as the health of the Body; nonparticipation undermines both and is not a biblical option.

Although it can be difficult for you to find your place in the church as a single mom, the reality of your place of belonging is not based on feelings but on fact. The cross reminds us of the price Jesus paid to secure this place of belonging for us. God's outrageous idea in the plan of redemption was to create an amazing organism, the Church—knit together, filled and empowered by the Spirit to embody His life, His love and His purposes on earth until Jesus Christ returns. At the foot of the cross you have been made whole; in Christ, each "whole one" makes a vital contribution to the greater whole of His Church.

A PLACE OF BELONGING

Just as our bodies have many parts and each part has a special function,
so it is with Christ's body. We are many parts of one body, and we all belong
to each other. In his grace, God has given us different gifts
for doing certain things well.
ROMANS 12:4-6, *NLT*

The human body has many parts, but the many parts make up one whole body. So it is with the body of Christ. . . . And if the ear says, "I am not part of the body because I am not an eye," would that make it any less a part of the body? . . . The eye can never say to the hand, "I don't need you." The head can't say to the feet, "I don't need you." In fact, some parts of the body that seem weakest and least important are actually the most necessary. . . . All of you together are Christ's body, and each of you is a part of it.
1 CORINTHIANS 12:12,16,20-22,27, *NLT*

God, for whom and through whom everything was made, chose to bring many children into glory. . . . So now Jesus and the ones he makes holy have the same Father. That is why Jesus is not ashamed to call them his brothers and sisters.
HEBREWS 2:10-11, *NLT*

Let us think of ways to motivate one another to acts of love and good works. And let us not neglect our meeting together, as some people do, but encourage one another, especially now that the day of his return is drawing near.
HEBREWS 10:24-25, *NLT*

FOR REFLECTION

You belong to an eternal family in which you are supernaturally and uniquely gifted for God's purposes. Embracing your place of belonging in this extended family will also shape your children's concept of the Church and their place of belonging in God's family.

LIVING AT A PLACE NEAR HIS ALTAR

What challenges do you face in finding your place in the church?

What are your spiritual gifts? (If you are not sure, consider using a spiritual gifts assessment tool online, such as www.buildingchurch.net).

What are manageable ways you can participate in your local church during this demanding season of single parenting?

INVITING YOUR CHILDREN TO HIS ALTAR

How can you rearrange your weekly schedule to facilitate your children's regular participation in worship, Sunday School, youth group or other activities at your local church?

Help your children build relationships with individuals in the Body who are spiritually mature, healthy role models—perhaps a youth leader, a teacher or a caring young adult.

Affirm gifts you see in your children (e.g., giving, serving, compassion, encouragement) and brainstorm ways they can use these gifts to serve the Church.

PRAYER NOTES AND PERSONAL REFLECTIONS

LONELINESS

Finding Daily Companionship with God

Subject line: Whining. A three-sentence email to another single mom was enough; I just needed to vent. "Today I'm having an I'm-tired-of-being-single-handling-everything-myself day. Just needed to whine to someone who gets it. I hope your day is going better than mine!" Beth sent her condolences, noting that some days you just want to go back to bed and pull the sheets over your head. She understood how pangs of loneliness could emotionally derail an entire day.

Savoring the idea of melting into my mattress, my thoughts drifted to the picture hanging above my bed. It is "bad art" by all accounts; my artist friends would gag if they saw it. But for me, its appeal is in its story. It was a garage sale find after my divorce, just before my move to Texas. Moving presented an opportunity to turn "our" bedroom into "my" bedroom. Stopping at a garage sale, I looked around for an inexpensive picture to hang above my bed. A large print of a garden scene caught my eye. It wasn't anything extraordinary, but the size was right, the colors worked and the price was unbeatable! Several weeks later, after hanging the picture in my new bedroom, I was pleased to see it pull the whole room together.

The painful transition of leaving friends behind, of starting my daughters off in new schools and looking for a new church accentuated my feelings of fear, inadequacy and especially my profound, aching loneliness. At one church I visited, the preacher's words exposed the almost palpable hole in my soul as he extended God's invitation to "a table set for two." I craved that intimacy—with God, or with anyone. The next morning, Bible in hand, I curled up in my chair in the corner of my bedroom. Pouring out my heart to the Lord, I sank into His strong, loving embrace, and water from the Rock washed over the dry, broken ground of my soul. Yes, He had "prepare[d] a table before me in the presence of my enemies" (Psalm 23:5). The "enemies" of discouragement, loneliness, fear and inadequacy scuttled away as I basked in the light of God's unchanging promises: "I will never leave you nor forsake you" (Joshua 1:5); "I have loved you with an everlasting love" (Jeremiah 31:3); "Do not fear, for I am with you . . . I will strengthen you and help you" (Isaiah 41:10). I knew afresh that my deepest longings could only be fully satisfied in Him.

Lifting my bowed head, I noticed the picture above my bed, and gasped. Prominent in the foreground of the garden scene was a table, set for two. A teapot hinted at the warm fellowship anticipated there. Silent tears coursed down my cheeks as I sensed that this garage sale "find" had been earmarked for me—a visual reminder each morning in my easy chair and each night as I put my head on my pillow that I am not alone. God is present in each moment, waiting to enjoy sweet companionship with me at a table set for two.

The altar in the Temple, in the Old Testament, was a "table" for sacrifices, establishing communion with God, foreshadowing the final altar of the cross of Christ. *This is my body, broken for you; take, eat. . . . This is my blood, spilled for the forgiveness of sin; take; drink. . . . I am going away, but I will not abandon you; my Spirit will come, to be with you and be in you.* It doesn't get any more intimate than that; union with Him is true communion. The companionship my soul most deeply craves is found at the foot of the cross. There, I also find a circle of interdependent relationships in His Body that provide mutual emotional and spiritual support.

One day several years after my move, I took a closer look at the picture above my bed. Below the artist's name was the title "Through God's Grace." My eyes filled with tears again. Yes, although I sometimes feel lonely, through God's grace I have not been alone; I have found deep intimacy with One who is loving, faithful, sufficient and strong. I have learned that pangs of loneliness are usually soul-hunger pangs telling me I have not spent enough time at this table set for two. Through God's grace, He invites me daily to this place of sweet communion purchased and permanently reserved for me by the precious blood of Jesus.

A PLACE OF CELEBRATING GOD'S PRESENCE

*Why spend money on what is not bread, and your labor
on what does not satisfy? Listen, listen to me, and eat what is good,
and your soul will delight in the richest of fare. Give ear and come
to me; hear me, that your soul may live. I will make an everlasting
covenant with you, my faithful love promised to David.*
ISAIAH 55:2-3

*Then Jesus declared, "I am the bread of life.
He who comes to me will never go hungry, and he who
believes in me will never be thirsty."*
JOHN 6:35

*And I will ask the Father, and he will give you another Counselor
to be with you forever—the Spirit of truth. The world cannot accept him,
because it neither sees him nor knows him. But you know him, for he
lives with you and will be in you.*
JOHN 14:16-17

*Look! I stand at the door and knock. If you hear my voice and open the door,
I will come in, and we will share a meal together as friends.*
REVELATION 3:20, NLT

FOR REFLECTION

The cross of Christ opened up personal fellowship with God that exceeds and redefines any intimacy we have with others.

LIVING AT A PLACE NEAR HIS ALTAR

When are you most vulnerable to feeling lonely? How do you fill that void?

When and where do you meet with God?

Who are the people in your life who embody Christ's presence to you?

INVITING YOUR CHILDREN TO CELEBRATE HIS PRESENCE

Ask your children to identify times when they feel lonely; discuss appropriate and inappropriate ways to meet their relational needs.

Being present to your children is one way you embody Christ to them. Carve out regular one-on-one time for meaningful interaction—whether in the car, at bedtime or even with a regular "phone date." Listen well, hug often, and try to ignore the clock.

Read Luke 22:14-20, and explain the meaning of communion to your children.

PRAYER NOTES AND PERSONAL REFLECTIONS

EMPOWERMENT

The Mystery of Christ in You

When my husband and I separated, I was terrified of the future. I had more questions than answers, more fear than faith and more doubt than hope. I was sure of only one thing: I would never be able to manage raising three kids by myself. Single parenting seemed *impossible*. No matter how tired I was, it was up to me to field questions, run last-minute errands, fix broken toys, mend broken hearts, medicate aches and pains, mediate sibling squabbling, feed growling tummies, supervise homework projects and chase after the runaway dog. The loss of companionship in the challenges of parenting was profound.

Perhaps Moses felt a similar weight of responsibility as he led the Israelites from Egypt to the Promised Land. Every time he turned around, "the kids" were whining, complaining, ranting and rebelling: There's nothing good to eat. I'm thirsty. Are we there yet? How much longer? Why can't we go back to the way things used to be? For Moses, there was no end in sight; how did he keep going?

The Bible reveals two inner resources that empowered Moses. He cultivated the holy habit of going to the tent of meeting, where he regularly conversed with God "face to face, as a man speaks with his friend" (Exodus 33:11). We can only imagine how Moses was shored up by God's whispers of encouragement, wisdom, comfort, love and reassuring promises!

But even so, Moses wanted a companion. "You have been telling me, 'Lead these people,' but you have not let me know whom you will send with me" (Exodus 33:12). You don't expect me to do this alone, do you? Then he added, "And remember that this nation is your very own people" (v. 13, *NLT*). Don't forget these are YOUR children, God!

God didn't need reminding, but perhaps Moses did—and so do we. *Our* children are *God's* children, whom He has entrusted to us. We know, understand and love them imperfectly; but God knows, understands and loves them perfectly! God's response was the loving reassurance of the wisest, most reliable co-parent Moses could ever have: "My Presence will go with you, and I will give you rest" (v. 14). Likewise, God has given each of us a companion, a co-parent to consult with and share the burdens of each day: Himself.

When God first called Moses to deliver His people from Egypt (see Exodus 3), He promised to be with him. Now He added another promise: "I will give you rest." Rest: the desire of every weary single parent! When do we get to the "rest" part? Rest comes when we rely on God's presence, operate out of His power and obediently walk in His paths. This "rest" is not the absence of external motion but the absence of internal commotion. "Rest" is the quieting of our souls as a child is quieted in her mother's arms.

Jesus said, "Come to Me, all of you who are weary and carry heavy burdens, and I will give you rest" (Matthew 11:28, *NLT*). Jesus chose to be present with us in our humanity, experiencing physical limitations, emotional distress and spiritual dependence on the Father. On the altar of the cross, Jesus shouldered the ultimate burden for us—our sin. Is there any burden He will not carry for us?

Jesus gave us the most profound and extraordinary promise of His Presence: "I will come to you" (John 14:18). The Holy Spirit would be *with* us and *in* us, empowering us with His very Presence in the most intimate way. Paul calls this a "mystery": "Christ *in* you, the hope of glory" (Colossians 1:27, emphasis mine). As we yield to Him, the Indwelling Spirit works in us with the same power that raised Jesus from the dead!

And so, we can say with Paul, "I can do everything through Christ, who gives me strength" (Philippians 4:13, *NLT*). *Everything*, even single parenting; even "leading these people"—God's children and ours—day in and day out, to maturity in Christ.

A PLACE OF CELEBRATING GOD'S PRESENCE

*And I will ask the Father, and he will give you another Advocate,
who will never leave you. He is the Holy Spirit, who leads into all truth.
The world cannot receive him, because it isn't looking for him and
doesn't recognize him. But you know him, because he lives with
you now and later will be in you. No, I will not abandon you
as orphans—I will come to you.*
JOHN 14:16-18, *NLT*

*Jesus replied, "All who love me will do what I say. My Father will love them,
and we will come and make our home with each of them."*
JOHN 14:23, *NLT*

*I'm telling you these things while I'm still living with you. The Friend, the Holy
Spirit whom the Father will send at my request, will make everything plain to you.
He will remind you of all the things I have told you. I'm leaving you well and
whole. That's my parting gift to you. Peace. I don't leave you the way you're used
to being left—feeling abandoned, bereft. So don't be upset. Don't be distraught.*
JOHN 14:25-27, *THE MESSAGE*

*I also pray that you will understand the incredible greatness of
God's power for us who believe him. This is the same mighty power
that raised Christ from the dead and seated him in the place of honor
at God's right hand in the heavenly realms.*
EPHESIANS 1:19-20, *NLT*

FOR REFLECTION

As you cultivate the holy habit of conversing with God "as with a friend," His Presence will encourage you and His rest will refresh you.

LIVING AT A PLACE NEAR HIS ALTAR

How can you incorporate Moses' habit of talking with God friend-to-friend into your life?

What keeps you from experiencing the "rest" God has promised?

Who are the godly people you know who can help shoulder your burden as a single mom?

INVITING YOUR CHILDREN TO HIS ALTAR

When your children feel overwhelmed, encourage them to pray. Remind them that the Holy Spirit's name is "the Helper."

When does God seem "present" or "absent" to your children? How does the promise of His presence wherever they are make a difference in their lives?

Who are the wise people in your children's lives who can help nurture them in Christ-likeness?

PRAYER NOTES AND PERSONAL REFLECTIONS

_____

_____

_____

_____

_____

_____

_____

_____

_____

_____

_____

_____

_____

SERVICE

All Ground Is Holy Ground

Gone are the days when I was a room mom and super-involved at my kids' school; that was my "other life," pre-divorce. Gone, too, are the hours on end when I was immersed in leading various women's ministries. That was my "work," though unpaid. With divorce came lifestyle changes and a paradigm shift. Now I am somewhat detached from the hub of activity in those previous arenas. Initially, I felt like an old broken horse put out to pasture, no longer terribly useful to God. Many single moms I know feel like that.

Moses also experienced a paradigm shift. In his "other life," he enjoyed a position of influence in Egypt as the adopted son of Pharaoh's daughter. But through a series of incidents, choices and unhappy endings, Moses ended up in Midian, shepherding sheep on the far side of the desert—isolated instead of influential; insignificant instead of important. But then God ignited an ordinary bush with His blazing glory, and the backside of beyond became "holy ground." *Kick your shoes off and listen to Me!* God presented Himself to Moses, and Moses reciprocated: "Here I am."

Moses was in for yet another paradigm shift: God planned to use Moses' ordinary skills for holy purposes—not by taking Moses *out* of the wilderness, but by using him *in* the wilderness. For years, he had shepherded stubborn, straying, not-so-smart sheep; now he would shepherd "God's sheep." Moses' initial protests of inadequacy were countered with God's simple but all-encompassing promise: "I will be with you" (Exodus 3:12). With God present, wherever Moses went would be "holy ground." His shepherd's staff, empowered by the Lord Almighty, would become the "staff of God," an instrument for miracles (see Exodus 3:2; 4:20). Stepping past his fears, Moses stepped into

God's plan, responding in faith and obedience, and embarked on the adventure of a lifetime.

Centuries later, wherever the God-man Jesus went, all ground became "holy ground." The ordinary venues of everyday life—hillsides, dusty streets, marketplaces or fishing boats—became His platform to display God's power and preach the Good News. By Jesus' willing, faithful obedience, an ordinary wooden cross became the altar of God, miraculously imparting eternal life to all who believe (see John 3:16).

Whatever ordinary work we do, whatever ordinary skills we possess, whatever ordinary tools are in our hands, God will use them all for His own holy purposes as we respond to Him in faith and obedience. Jesus' parting words included a simple promise, the only promise we need to accomplish His work: "And be sure of this: I am with you always, even to the end of the age" (Matthew 28:20, *NLT*). In my office, I am keenly aware that because of God's presence and power, I am on "holy ground," and the work He has given me is "holy work." During sessions with my clients, I envision Christ sitting in my extra chair and silently invite Him to be at work. Often, He shows up in unexpected, exciting ways! At times, it's tempting to slip off my shoes and revel in His Presence.

Where has God placed you, and what is in your hand?

A PLACE OF CELEBRATING GOD'S PRESENCE

The Lord replied, "I will personally go with you, Moses, and I will give you rest— everything will be fine for you." Then Moses said, "If you don't personally go with us, don't make us leave this place. How will anyone know that you look favorably on me—on me and on your people—if you don't go with us? For your presence among us sets your people and me apart from all other people on the earth."
EXODUS 33:14-16, *NLT*

One day as Jesus was walking along the shore of the Sea of Galilee, he saw two brothers—Simon, also called Peter, and Andrew—throwing a net into the water, for they fished for a living. Jesus called out to them, "Come, follow me, and I will show you how to fish for people!"
MATTHEW 4:18-19, *NLT*

Servants, respectfully obey your earthly masters but always with an eye to obeying the real master, Christ. Don't just do what you have to do to get by, but work heartily, as Christ's servants doing what God wants you to do. And work with a smile on your face, always keeping in mind that no matter who happens to be giving the orders, you're really serving God. Good work will get you good pay from the Master, regardless of whether you are slave or free.
EPHESIANS 6:5-8, *THE MESSAGE*

And whatever you do, whether in word or deed, do it all in the name of the Lord Jesus, giving thanks to God the Father through him.
COLOSSIANS 3:17

FOR REFLECTION

As Christians, we carry the Indwelling Christ into the world; whatever our work, it is His place of ministry and our offering to Him.

LIVING AT A PLACE NEAR HIS ALTAR

What kind of paradigm shift have you experienced as a single mom?

What is your "wilderness," and how might God use your wilderness experience for His own purposes?

How does God's promise, "I will be with you," change your perspective about your workplace?

What gifts, skills and tools of your trade can you offer God to use for His purposes?

INVITING YOUR CHILDREN TO HIS ALTAR

What challenges, difficulties or losses have your children experienced? How have these losses impacted their beliefs about themselves, life or

God? Relate the story of Exodus, noting both difficulties the children of Israel experienced, and ways that God took care of them.

Remind your children that God doesn't live at church; wherever they go, Jesus goes with them—to school, on the playing field and in their extracurricular activities. How does His presence make a difference in their attitudes, choices and behaviors?

Affirm your child's gifts and skills as gifts from God to be used for God. Share an example of how God has used something you consider ordinary for His own extraordinary purposes.

PRAYER NOTES AND PERSONAL REFLECTIONS

TRUST

Relying on God's Faithfulness to His Promises

Gorgeous flowers, beautiful music, soft candlelight. It was a picture-perfect wedding . . . *too* perfect. In the aftermath of my divorce, rose-colored glasses were no longer part of my guest-of-the-wedding attire; they clashed with the harsh colors of my reality. I winced as the bride and groom pledged their unconditional love to one another. As their covenant promises carved out expectations and fed their hopes of living happily ever after, it felt like a knife had been plunged into my stomach and turned. *They have no idea what these vows will require of them in the future. How can she reasonably trust he will keep his promises? Are promises, like rules, made to be broken?*

Marriage is a risky bargain. Weddings don't come with warranties; lifetime promises don't come with lifetime guarantees. Pledges of love and faithfulness are only as reliable as the fallible individuals who make them. What demonstrates trustworthiness is consistent action over time.

In the Old Testament, God often referred to Himself as "the God of Abraham, Isaac, and Jacob." He didn't ask for blind trust; instead, He stirred up their memory of past generations that had received His promises, walked in His ways and seen His consistent, faithful action on their behalf. In the Bible, many of God's promises come with unconditional guarantees: "You will be my people and I will be your God." Period. "Never again will I destroy the earth with a flood." Period. "Believe on the Lord Jesus Christ, and you will be saved." Period. These promises are rooted in God's unconditional love and unchanging character.

But God made other promises conditional, hinging them on the faith and obedience of His people. If His people stayed on course, then they would see His provision and blessing; if they deliberately charted their own course, then they would experience the consequences of their choices and miss the fulfillment of those promises. God's "if . . . then" promises are unequivocal but not unconditional. They were the result of His love but predicated on the freedom of choice that characterizes a mutual love relationship. God's love woos us but does not coerce our faith and obedience. He wants our hearts.

In either case, the promises of the Bible are as reliable as the One who made them. God has revealed His faithful character to anyone who observes His creation (see Romans 1:19-20). I can count on Him to keep His promises as surely as I can count on the sunrise (see Psalm 130:5-6). His faithfulness to His Word is as reliable as gravity, the seasons, the tides. All of these were spoken into creation and sustained by the power of His Word (see Colossians 1:16-17).

The biblical account, penned over the span of centuries, records the faithfulness of the God of Abraham, Isaac and Jacob. Keeping His promise to send a Messiah to His people, God took on flesh. He kept His promise all the way to the cross, where He sealed His pledge of love with His own blood. Three days later, He walked out of the tomb, keeping His promise to overcome the power of sin and death. He has kept His promises ever since by offering resurrection life through the Holy Spirit to anyone who asks. All of God's promises are "yes" to us in Christ Jesus (see 2 Corinthians 1:20). *All* of them.

Now when I attend weddings, I am reminded of my promise-making/promise-keeping God who pledged His unfailing love to me on the altar of the cross, and who desires my unfailing love in return. His promises to me are reliable, although mine to Him are not. By His grace, I definitely get the better end of the bargain in this risky love relationship. It is truly a marriage made in heaven.

How can I trust His promises in the face of an unknown future? *His consistent action over time demonstrates His trustworthiness.*

A PLACE OF CELEBRATING GOD'S PROMISES

You know with all your heart and soul that not one of all the good promises the Lord your God gave you has failed. Every promise has been fulfilled; not one has failed.
JOSHUA 23:14

God's way is perfect. All the LORD's promises prove true. He is a shield for all who look to him for protection.
PSALM 18:30, *NLT*

Then I will praise you with music on the harp, because you are faithful to your promises, O my God. I will sing praises to you with a lyre, O Holy One of Israel.
PSALM 71:22, *NLT*

Your promises have been thoroughly tested; that is why I love them so much.
PSALM 119:140, *NLT*

I bow before your holy Temple as I worship. I praise your name for your unfailing love and faithfulness; for your promises are backed by all the honor of your name.
PSALM 138:2, *NLT*

For all of God's promises have been fulfilled in Christ with a resounding "Yes!" And through Christ, our "Amen" (which means "Yes") ascends to God for his glory.
2 CORINTHIANS 1:20, *NLT*

And because of his glory and excellence, he has given us great and precious promises. These are the promises that enable you to share his divine nature and escape the world's corruption caused by human desires. In view of all this, make every effort to respond to God's promises.
2 PETER 1:4-5, *NLT*

FOR REFLECTION

The promises of our faithful God are backed with His Word, upheld by His unchanging character, sealed with the blood of His own Son and guaranteed in full by the Holy Spirit.

LIVING AT A PLACE NEAR HIS ALTAR

How well do you know the One who pledged His love to you on the altar of the cross?

What has God promised you? What risks are there in trusting His promises?

How have you seen Him keep His promises to you thus far?

INVITING YOUR CHILDREN TO HIS ALTAR

Who does your child consider trustworthy?

How does this person model Christ to your children?

What do TV advertisements promise? Are those trustworthy promises?

Teach your children the value of integrity by keeping promises you make and holding them to their promises. Challenge them to be cautious promise makers and loyal promise keepers.

PRAYER NOTES AND PERSONAL REFLECTIONS

_____

_____

_____

_____

_____

_____

_____

_____

_____

_____

DISAPPOINTMENT

Identifying What God Has Promised You

The cardboard box provided a makeshift nest for four tiny bunnies, each one smaller than the palm of my hand. Ten-year-old Robin, lover of all creatures great and small, discovered them abandoned in our back yard. She was determined to give them a fighting chance at life. Over the next week, Robin kept vigil—feeding them through a dropper, stroking them, *willing* them to live. It was heartbreaking to watch, really. Sometimes devotion and determination aren't enough to overcome factors beyond our control. *This isn't going to end well,* I thought. Although I wanted to be supportive, what I really wanted was to shield her from yet another disappointment in life. *Don't love them too much, Robin.*

"I can't believe it!" we groan, shaking our heads in disappointment. Events, people, organizations—we can be disappointed by any and all of these things. Sometimes we are disappointed with ourselves; sometimes we are disappointed with God. He didn't do what we hoped He would; or, perhaps it seems as if He didn't do anything—the greatest let-down of all. The disbelief embedded in our reaction to disappointment reveals our ill-founded presumptions and unmet expectations.

After a couple years of infertility, my miraculous first pregnancy ended abruptly in miscarriage. I was *devastated*. No explanation from God would have comforted me at the time; I just wanted that baby. Early the next morning, I struggled with Romans 5:5: "Hope does not disappoint us, because God has poured out his love into our hearts by the Holy Spirit." *That doesn't ring true with my experience; I am disappointed, and I don't feel God's love.* A phone call interrupted my thoughts. Dad's voice cracked as he told me through tears how sorry he was about the miscarriage, and how much he loved me. His call was so unusual; Dad rarely called without Mom; he didn't often say, "I love you"; and he never cried. I wept as I felt his long-distance embrace. In the moment that I could not feel my heavenly Father's love, it seemed He "put skin on," loving me through my earthly father.

Hanging up the phone, a tune I vaguely remembered from my childhood niggled at the back of my mind. I leafed through an old hymnal until I found it: "All the Way My Savior Leads Me." The lyrics stunned me:

All the way my Savior leads me; What have I to ask beside?
Can I doubt His tender mercy, Who through life has been my Guide?
Heav'nly peace, divinest comfort, Here by faith in Him to dwell!
For I know, whate'er befall me, Jesus doeth all things well;
For I know, whate'er befall me, Jesus doeth all things well.

The words massaged my soul, and the early morning chain of events assured me that God was present, though He seemed absent. In the midst of my disappointment, God showed me His love in unexpected ways. Instead of giving me explanations, He comforted me with His love and His promises.

God never promised me a baby, then or in the future. But I began to hold on to what He *had* promised: His utter faithfulness and new mercies each day (see Lamentations 3:22-23); the "Comforter"—to meet me where words fail and tears run out (see John 16:6-7,33); His sovereign control holding everything together, even when it seems my world is falling apart (see Psalm 46). Ultimately, He promised me Himself, through the love of Jesus Christ and the power of the indwelling Holy Spirit.

Those lessons proved invaluable over the years ahead, and particularly when my marriage disintegrated. No divine explanations would have given me understanding or comfort at the time. But identifying what God had—and had not—promised gave me well-founded and realistic expectations of Him. God never promised that my marriage would be restored. Instead, He promised to restore *me*—a promise He has kept faithfully. God always keeps His promises, even though perhaps in unexpected ways.

At the foot of the cross we see the most extraordinary fulfillment of God's promises, the ultimate expression of His love—sending His beloved Son to be our Savior. Because of Jesus' death and resurrection, our hope in God is *not* disappointed; rather, His love invades and permeates every corner of our lives and meets us in every unexpected circumstance through the power of the Holy Spirit.

Yes, the bunnies died. Despite her disappointment, Robin's efforts were not wasted; loving with devotion and compassion is worthwhile, regardless of the outcome. It was a good life lesson, reflecting the way she has been loved by her heavenly Father. *Don't be afraid to love well, Robin.*

A PLACE OF CELEBRATING GOD'S PROMISES

God is not a man, that he should lie, nor a son of man, that he should change his mind. Does he speak and then not act? Does he promise and not fulfill?
NUMBERS 23:19

They cried to you and were saved; in you they trusted and were not disappointed.
PSALM 22:5

My soul, wait only upon God and silently submit to Him; for my hope and expectation are from Him. He only is my Rock and my Salvation; He is my Defense and my Fortress, I shall not be moved.
PSALM 62:5-6, AMP

We can rejoice, too, when we run into problems and trials, for we know that they help us develop endurance. And endurance develops strength of character, and character strengthens our confident hope of salvation. And this hope will not lead to disappointment. For we know how dearly God loves us, because he has given us the Holy Spirit to fill our hearts with his love.
ROMANS 5:3-5, NLT

FOR REFLECTION

Instead of protecting us from disappointment, God meets us there with His promises, giving us hope within and beyond our circumstances.

LIVING AT A PLACE NEAR HIS ALTAR

What expectations were hidden underneath disappointments you have experienced?

What expectations do you have of God?

What has He promised you in your present circumstances?

INVITING YOUR CHILDREN TO HIS ALTAR

When your children are disappointed, respond with empathy and compassion. Relate a similar disappointment you experienced, and how you felt at the time.

Rather than protect your children from potential disappointments, help them anticipate possible outcomes and learn to make choices with their eyes wide open, weighing both risks and benefits.

How were the disciples disappointed when Jesus was crucified? How did God fulfill His promises on the cross? On a paper cross bookmark, write a promise your children can claim in a current disappointment.

PRAYER NOTES AND PERSONAL REFLECTIONS

_____

_____

_____

_____

_____

_____

_____

_____

_____

_____

_____

DAY 15

❖

DISCOURAGEMENT

Finding Comfort and Hope in God's Promises

"I feel like Daddy doesn't love me anymore." Amanda's tears cascaded down her cheeks as her mom pulled her small body close. *How do you swaddle a seven-year-old?* It had been almost a year since Amanda's father had cut off all contact with the children; Rachel's heartache for her kids was a dull, daily undercurrent of pain that never quit. The deficit in the checking account created by missed child-support checks was marginal in comparison to the growing hole in her children's hearts.

On the surface, the kids were keeping up a good front, maintaining strong grades and participating in school and youth group activities. But Rachel saw what was happening to their hearts. Courtney's was chasing affirmation from her boyfriend. Allison's heart was crumbling, evidenced by significant weight loss and emotional withdrawal. Brent's was hardening around the edges; a snippy, critical attitude displaced his usual cheerfulness. And little Amanda's heart questioned her value and significance, undermining her confidence socially. Their father's abandonment of relationship added yet another layer of pain to the ongoing toll of divorce. *How could their father hurt his own children this way?*

Hugging Amanda, Rachel felt discouraged; she had more questions than answers these days. Was the God who fills the universe big enough to fill the void in her children's' hearts? In creation, He made something "very good" out of nothing; could He make something "very good" out of their emptiness too? Would the God who cradles the earth in the palm of His hand hold them just as securely, keeping their lives from spinning completely out of control? God set boundaries on the ocean waters; would He also limit the pain that seemed to flood their lives? Would the One who pulled the mountains out of dust fashion something strong and beautiful out of the residue in their lives?

As Rachel probed the unknown, God's promises quickly tumbled into her mind on top of each question:

> I will be a Father to the fatherless; in every way, every day. That is My promise to you and to your children. I will never leave them or forsake them; I will not abandon them physically, emotionally or spiritually. I carry their wounds in My own heart; I felt their pain on the cross where I was wounded and rejected by sinful men. As surely as I weep with them and count their tears, I will wipe their tears with My nail-pierced hands and restore their joy. I will give them a future and a hope, because I hold the future, and I am Hope. I will do more than you ask or even think, because I Am God; nothing is too difficult for Me. I love your children with an everlasting love that is higher than the mountains, deeper than the sea, more constant than the sunrise, more encompassing than the air you breathe (see Psalm 68:5; Deuteronomy 31:8; Isaiah 53:3-4; Psalm 56:8; Jeremiah 29:11; Ephesians 3:18,20; Jeremiah 31:3; 2 Corinthians 1:20).

Even as circumstances drained her emotionally, God's promises administered spiritual CPR. Yes, *Claiming Promises Resuscitates*. As Rachel inhaled hope and exhaled discouragement, she held Amanda tightly, stroking her hair and silently praying. Then Rachel began to give spiritual CPR to Amanda, speaking the truth about her heavenly Father. "I know it feels like Daddy doesn't love you, and I'm so sorry. You have a heavenly Father who loves you more than you can ever imagine. I have asked Him to fill the empty places in your heart, and I'm counting on Him to do so. I don't know what's going on with Daddy, but I know your heavenly Father is right here, every day, loving you, holding you, helping you, blessing you. He is never going to let go; He promised. Hold on to Him tight, sweetie." Amanda relaxed in Rachel's arms, soothed and comforted by her heavenly Father's promises.

On the cross, the Promised One fulfilled God's promises and brought healing love to a world broken by sinful choices. Light penetrated darkness; hope overcame despair; and life swallowed up death. Forever. All the promises of God are "yes" to us, and to our children, through Christ Jesus.

A PLACE OF CELEBRATING GOD'S PROMISES

Remember what you said to me, your servant—I hang on to these words for dear life! These words hold me up in bad times; yes, your promises rejuvenate me.
PSALM 119:49, *THE MESSAGE*

I rise before dawn and cry for help; I have put my hope in your word. My eyes stay open through the watches of the night, that I may meditate on your promises.
PSALM 119:147-148

The LORD is faithful to all his promises and loving toward all he has made.
PSALM 145:13

Abraham never wavered in believing God's promise. In fact, his faith grew stronger, and in this he brought glory to God. He was fully convinced that God is able to do whatever he promises. And because of Abraham's faith, God counted him as righteous.
ROMANS 4:20-22, *NLT*

For all of God's promises have been fulfilled in Christ with a resounding "Yes!" And through Christ, our "Amen" (which means "Yes") ascends to God for his glory.
2 CORINTHIANS 1:20, *NLT*

FOR REFLECTION

In every discouraging moment, we are encouraged—"filled with courage"—by God's promises, because He is with us and He is greater than our circumstances.

LIVING AT A PLACE NEAR HIS ALTAR

In what area(s) are you battling discouragement in your life right now?

What questions do you want to ask God about the situation?

What promise can you claim in the face of discouragement?

INVITING YOUR CHILDREN TO HIS ALTAR

Discouragement wears many disguises: irritability, whining, sluggishness, passivity. Find out what negative feelings are hiding underneath your child's behavior. Listen with empathy, without minimizing or "fixing" the problem.

Ask your kids to scan the horizon. What blocks their view? What is beyond their view? Remind them that God sees beyond our circumstances and is greater than our problems, no matter how big they seem.

Create a deck of "Promise Cards." On one side write an emotion (discouragement, fear, worry, disappointment, doubt); on the other side, write a promise from God. On a difficult day, tuck a promise card in your child's lunch, coat pocket or under his or her pillow.

PRAYER NOTES AND PERSONAL REFLECTIONS

_____

_____

_____

_____

_____

_____

_____

_____

_____

_____

DAY 16

VULNERABILITY

Living in Freedom from the Emotional Traps of the Enemy

I felt utterly vulnerable. In the days immediately following my separation from my husband, my head was spinning, my emotions churning and my heart had shattered into a gazillion little pieces. I had more questions than answers—about my life and about God. The One who could have protected me and prevented my present circumstances seemingly stood by and watched from a distance while my world caved in and collapsed. In this minefield of pain and confusion, I had to make a choice: to rely on the One who had allowed the unthinkable or to venture into the dark, uncharted territory of my family's future, relying on my own wits. Life did not feel safe anymore; I needed a Hand to hold, even if my faith felt wobbly. My theological quandary would have to take a backseat for the time being. The resolve of the psalmist in Psalm 31, simultaneously seeking and claiming refuge in God, bolstered my fearful, faltering spirit.

It was verse 4 that stopped me in my tracks: "Free me from the trap that is set for me, for you are my refuge." Who prays for freedom *before* he is entrapped? David did. Having been outwitted by his enemy in the past, he humbly acknowledged his vulnerability. He sought refuge from mortal enemies and presumed he would be unsuspectingly ensnared by them. But the archenemy of my soul, Satan, was much more sinister. He had already gained territory and wreaked havoc in my marriage; when I surveyed the damage, I felt angry and determined to not let Satan gain an inch more territory in me or in our home. All too easily, I could become entangled in the subtle, sticky web of his manipulations to gain a foothold in my soul.

What were the traps set for me? The long, ugly list filled a full page in my journal: bitterness, resentment, fear, doubt, hopelessness, despair, depression, anxiety, hostility, vindictiveness, hatred, revenge, contempt, slander, self-pity, self-righteousness, selfishness, pride, entitlement, rationalizing . . . any of these toxic traps, given the opportunity, would undermine my relationship with God and my ability to lead my children in the months ahead. It was an ugly list to read, much less own. At the foot of the cross, I asked the Lord to expose and uproot any insidious attitudes that were beginning to choke His life out of me—for my sake, for the sake of my children and for the sake of His name.

Daily self-examination revealed my susceptibility to Satan's cunning maneuvers and required that I keep short accounts with God. At times, the unwelcome guests of fear, doubt, anxiety or self-pity would assault me without warning. But when I ran to my Refuge, they would be kept in check. When I felt misunderstood, misrepresented, misjudged or mistreated by others, I brought my fleshly reactions to the foot of the cross, where my Savior empathized with me. My daily plea "Free me from the trap that is set for me" became a shield, deflecting the poisoned arrows of the enemy.

Sometimes I was completely ambushed by emotional land mines; other times, I foolishly, bullishly, blindly walked head-on into visible traps. Whimpering and limping to my Refuge, I found comfort, forgiveness, encouragement and renewed strength. Surrendering my weaknesses and vulnerability to Him at the foot of the cross, my place of Refuge gradually became a place of freedom as God empowered me to recognize traps in advance, create boundaries to sidestep emotional land mines, and embrace His peace. As I have relied on my Refuge in utter dependence, He has proved Himself completely faithful.

A PLACE OF REFUGE

Sin is crouching at the door, eager to control you.
But you must subdue it and be its master.
GENESIS 4:7, *NLT*

In you, O LORD, I have taken refuge; let me never be put to shame;
deliver me in your righteousness. Turn your ear to me, come quickly to my rescue;
be my rock of refuge, a strong fortress to save me. Since you are my rock and my
fortress, for the sake of your name lead and guide me.
Free me from the trap that is set for me, for you are my refuge.
PSALM 31:1-4

But the LORD is my fortress; my God is the mighty rock where I hide.
PSALM 94:22, *NLT*

Give all your worries and cares to God, for he cares about you. Stay alert! Watch out for your great enemy, the devil. He prowls around like a roaring lion, looking for someone to devour. Stand firm against him, and be strong in your faith.
1 PETER 5:7-9, *NLT*

You, dear children, are from God and have overcome them, because the one who is in you is greater than the one who is in the world.
1 JOHN 4:4

FOR REFLECTION

Recognizing our vulnerabilities requires attentiveness in our relationships and circumstances. We do not need to live in fear of our enemy; we must be wise and alert to maintain our advantage over him through the power of the Holy Spirit.

LIVING AT A PLACE NEAR YOUR ALTAR

Make a list of the "traps" or emotional land mines set for you in your present circumstances.

Usually our self-protective tactics prove to be self-defeating. How would your responses to these "traps" be different if you relied on God as your Refuge?

What do you need to surrender to God today to truly rely on Him?

INVITING YOUR CHILDREN TO HIS ALTAR

Play a game with your children that requires strategy to win (e.g., checkers). Discuss the strategies they use to win and what happens if they are careless. Relate this to temptations they face, and discuss strategies for overcoming temptation.

Tell your children about a "trap" you fall into, and ask them to identify "traps" they struggle with, such as fear, worry, arguing, and so on. Buy a 25-cent mouse trap at the hardware store (remove the spring to avoid injury); glue a magnet on the backside and print Psalm 31:4 on the front. Place the "trap magnet" on your refrigerator; each week insert an attitude or behavior (written on one-inch-by-one-inch paper) under the catch of the trap as a reminder to be alert.

Paul reminds us that the Word of God is our offensive weapon against the enemy (see Ephesians 6:17). Pray God's Word with your children related to the daily struggles they face. Remind them that through Jesus Christ, they are on the winning side of the battle!

PRAYER NOTES AND PERSONAL REFLECTIONS

INSECURITY

Finding Security in the Palm of God's Hand

Dog-tired, stretched for patience and feeling emotionally threadbare, it was tempting to forgo my four-year-old's elongated bedtime rituals. But I knew this one-on-one time was essential. Cuddling, recapping the day, reading a Bible story and praying together provided the comfort of routine—though barely masking the reality that nothing was normal anymore.

I knew that her father's absence was confusing to her; I could hardly wrap my own mind around it. What did she think about as she snuggled up with her favorite baby blanket after lights-out? Emily seemed so small and vulnerable. Wanting to somehow shore up her sense of security, I added a new ritual: each evening after praying together, I put her small hand in mine and pointed to her open palm. "Emily, you are right there, in the palm of God's hand. You are going to be okay, because He wraps His love around you like a blanket, holds you and is taking care of you." I would close her short fingers into a little fist, hoping that holding on to the truth would give her a small measure of comfort as she drifted off to sleep. Whether or not the ritual helped her, it helped *me* to remember that our fragile lives were in God's strong hands.

The unpredictability of life events and our inability to control what happens leaves us all feeling vulnerable. Emily is in middle school now; today they had a "lockdown drill." The drills create preparedness by instilling knowledge, raising confidence and practicing habits so that in the event of a crisis, fear and panic will not result in utter pandemonium. Hopefully, everyone will reflexively run to their place of safety and stay put, quiet and still.

Where do you reflexively run when you feel vulnerable?

In response to the unpredictability of life, David developed the holy habit of running to his Refuge when chased by mortal enemies, emotional struggles or spiritual battles. Reading the psalms is like reading his private journals; his prayers were riddled with themes of betrayal, loss, fear, anger, depression and anxiety. Repeatedly, he ran to his Refuge. He sorted out his doubt-filled questions and honest emotions in the safety of his relationship with God. Are your enemies of fear, discouragement or shame chasing you down? God says, *Come hide in Me.* Does anxiety have you on the run? *I am your place of safety.* Does life feel out of control? *Stay put, quiet and still.*

The apostle Paul, who lived with great adversity and persecution, reminds us, "you have been raised with Christ . . . your life is now hidden with Christ in God" (Colossians 3:1-4). That's heavy-duty theology, but the spiritual reality is as real as the tangible reality around me. This life Paul describes is not "pie in the sky when I die"; it is my true, present position in Christ as a child of God, a position secured for me by Christ on the cross.

In calm or in calamity, my life as a believer is enveloped in Christ, and Christ is in God. I can hide in the folds of His love and wrap myself in the blanket of His promises. Shielded by His faithfulness, I can hunker down in the security of His sovereign care. Hiding in my strong Fortress, I am in a place of emotional safety and spiritual freedom where I can squarely face my enemies: anxiety, doubt, fear or discouragement. They might do battle with me, but they cannot overcome me here. I am on the winning side and my Warrior-King does battle on my behalf as I hide myself in Him. This is the amazing, extraordinarily intimate and protective relationship that Jesus prayed for in Gethsemane the night before He hung on the cross (see John 17). Through His death and resurrection, we have been brought into oneness with the triune God. I cannot imagine a greater place of security for me or for my children. Can you?

A PLACE OF REFUGE

Let all that I am wait quietly before God, for my hope is in him. He alone is my rock and my salvation, my fortress where I will not be shaken. My victory and honor come from God alone. He is my refuge, a rock where no enemy can reach me. O my people, trust in him at all times. Pour out your heart to him, for God is our refuge.
PSALM 62:5-8, *NLT*

Because you are my helper, I sing for joy in the shadow of your wings.
I cling to you; your strong right hand holds me securely.
PSALM 63:7-8, *NLT*

Can a woman forget her nursing child and have no compassion on the son of
her womb? Even these may forget, but I will not forget you. Behold, I have
inscribed you on the palms of My hands; Your walls are continually before Me.
ISAIAH 49:15-16, *NASB*

For you died to this life, and your real life is hidden with
Christ in God. And when Christ, who is your life, is revealed to
the whole world, you will share in all his glory.
COLOSSIANS 3:3-4, *NLT*

FOR REFLECTION

Practicing daily the habit of turning to God in the "small stuff" of life prepares us to reflexively run to Him as our Refuge when the "big stuff" hits the fan.

LIVING AT A PLACE NEAR HIS ALTAR

When do you feel most vulnerable? What "enemies" taunt you?

How can you practice running to God as your refuge, even in the "small stuff"?

How does the truth that your life is "hidden with Christ in God" change your view of your circumstances?

INVITING YOUR CHILDREN TO HIS ALTAR

Play hide-and-seek with your children; players that are hiding from whoever is "IT" may run to "the Refuge" (home base) to keep from being tagged by "IT."

Ask your children to write a list of words describing themselves. Place each list in a letter-size envelope with the child's name on the outside. Seal that envelope in a legal-size envelope labeled "Jesus Christ." Place that envelope in a manila envelope labeled "God," and seal it. Use the envelopes to describe the security they have in their Refuge.

When your children express fears or worries, suggest, "Let's run to the Rock." Pray a short sentence prayer with them, developing the holy habit of turning to God.

PRAYER NOTES AND PERSONAL REFLECTIONS

_____

_____

_____

_____

_____

_____

_____

_____

_____

_____

_____

_____

_____

_____

_____

_____

_____

_____

_____

FEAR

Hiding in God in the Midst of Adversity

If I were standing, my knees would be buckling. Thankfully, I'm sitting down. Instead, my spirit is buckling. Fear scrambles my racing thoughts; I pray for my daughter without even knowing the words to say. *God, please heal her!* For four months, Robin has been battling a mysterious illness; every time she gets better, she relapses. This time around, her symptoms are worse, and the "ordinary" kinds of ailments have been ruled out. Robin feels frustrated, discouraged and distressed; I am fearful and worried. Scary words from the morning's conversation with her baffled doctor echo in my ears: *specialists, CT scans, nonmalignant tumors, biopsies* . . . and other words I don't know how to pronounce or spell. These are words I don't want to hear, especially when my daughter is a thousand miles away at college.

Dr. Rhonda, my dear friend and my daughter's doctor, gracefully switched hats throughout our consultation, relating to me both professionally and personally. "Do I need to come?" I asked, already mentally boarding a plane. "No, not yet; wait. Let me talk with the specialists today," Rhonda said reassuringly. So instead of running to my daughter, fear propels me to the Throne of Grace and I plead—for healing, for wisdom, for comfort.

I don't like carrying the weight of this alone. Today, walking solo is harder than hard—several notches above ordinary days that are challenging, tiring and taxing. I am blessed with a band of prayerful and supportive family and friends. But no one else is walking in my moccasins; no one else shares the yoke of this burden as a co-parent. Despite my circle of support, in many ways I feel profoundly alone today with the weight of my fears, concerns, and the medical decisions that I might face in the next 24 hours.

Psalm 46 breaks through my racing thoughts: "God is our refuge and strength, an ever-present help in trouble. Therefore we will not fear" (v. 1) . . . *even if the mountains are collapsing and the earth is quaking . . . even if my daughter is mysteriously and potentially seriously ill. God is my refuge in this ordeal; He is my present help in THIS trouble.*

Psalm 46, written by an unknown author and sung in worship at the Temple, celebrated the Lord Almighty's sovereign care, *no matter what happens.* The psalmist makes it obvious that having God as my Refuge doesn't mean my life will not be touched by bad or even horrible events; it means the very core of my true life will be protected and secure even in those events. As surely as the-God-who-is-in-control pledged His help to His beloved Jerusalem, His dwelling place (see v. 4), I can trust that He will help me, for now He dwells in me by His Spirit. "God is within her, she will not fall; God will help her at break of day" (v. 5). Yes, no matter what each new day brings.

In the Psalms, David's frequent reference to God as his refuge, fortress and hiding place—safe, secure, comforting images—reflect David's habit of trust in God when his enemies were pursuing him. What is my habit in times of difficulty? Do I turn to God as my last resort, or do I turn to Him as my first resource?

Today, as my enemy of fear chases me down, I run to my Refuge, hold on tight and allow Him to hold me tight. Sputtering out my jumbled thoughts, God's strong embrace quiets me; I remember that I am not alone, and I do not bear the weight of my concerns alone. Jesus made sure of that on the cross. Bearing my sin, He suffered complete separation from the Father so that by His grace I would never be separated from Him. The cross and the resurrection stand as bookends of the most dramatic weekend in history, reminding me that even in seemingly godforsaken circumstances, the Lord Almighty has the upper hand. He is present, and He is powerful. His Spirit is not only with me but also within me. Counselor, Comforter and Helper are His names. My fears begin to subside. *God is our refuge and strength, an ever-present help in trouble.*

Robin and I are in good hands; we are in God's hands. In the uncertainties of life, there is no more secure place to be.

A Place of Refuge

*For you are my hiding place; you protect me from trouble. You surround
me with songs of victory. The Lord says, "I will guide you along the best pathway
for your life. I will advise you and watch over you."*
PSALM 32:7-8, NLT

*God is our refuge and strength, an ever-present help in trouble. . . .
The LORD Almighty is with us; the God of Jacob is our fortress.*
PSALM 46:1,7

*But as for me, I will sing about your power. Each morning I will sing with joy
about your unfailing love. For you have been my refuge, a place of safety when I
am in distress. O my Strength, to you I sing praises, for you, O God, are my
refuge, the God who shows me unfailing love.*
PSALM 59:16-17, NLT

*But you are a tower of refuge to the poor, O LORD, a tower of refuge to the needy
in distress. You are a refuge from the storm and a shelter from the heat.*
ISAIAH 25:4, NLT

*Don't be afraid, for I am with you. Don't be discouraged, for I am your God. I will
strengthen you and help you. I will hold you up with my victorious right hand.*
ISAIAH 41:10, NLT

For Reflection

We do not have to run far to our place of Refuge. By the grace of God,
through the cross of Christ, our Refuge is only a prayer away.

Living at a Place Near His Altar

When do you find it most difficult to walk the path of parenting
alone? *When the kids are expecting Dad
to be home. I can see the disappointment
in Natalie.*

Do you turn to God as your last resort or your first resource?

What promises does our Refuge give you? Select one of the Scriptures above to memorize.

INVITING YOUR CHILDREN TO HIS ALTAR

Listen to your children's fears related to: world events, school, friends, family. Relate similar fears that you have faced and how you overcame them.

Ask about a time when your child felt alone; did God seem near or far away?

From the section "A Place of Refuge," select a promise for each of your children. Write it on a note card and tuck it under their pillow for a bedtime surprise.

PRAYER NOTES AND PERSONAL REFLECTIONS

_____

_____

_____

_____

_____

_____

_____

_____

_____

_____

_____

_____

_____

_____

STRUGGLE

When You Don't Know How to Pray

My mind was overwhelmed and my body exhausted as I considered the day ahead. *I should pray, but I don't even know where to start!* An unexpected question popped into my head: *How would Jesus pray for me today?* I had no idea, but the thought of Him conversing with the Father about me throughout the day was comforting. Somehow, it gave me assurance that my crazy day would turn out okay.

When I was little, I loved listening to my mom play hymns on the piano after we were tucked in bed. It was her way of unwinding, and it became my way of unwinding as well, lulling me to sleep. If a key signature didn't suit her, she "shifted gears," transposing from sharps to flats. Her flourishes and embellishments interpreted and enhanced the blunt black notes in the hymnal, and it was beautiful. Sometimes, I would sneak out of bed, perch on the stairs and press my ear to the wall, just to listen better. The soothing sounds vibrating in the wall settled my soul, and eventually I would slip back upstairs to bed.

My prayers are like those blunt black notes: simple, choppy, bland, and often presented in the "key" of my mood or circumstances. Sometimes they are dissonant—a mixture of belief and unbelief. But when I pray in the name of Jesus, He transposes my stilted, shortsighted prayers according to His will, interceding for me with the Father. When I struggle for words, the Spirit translates my wordless groanings into the language of the Trinity and prays for me. Even prayer is something I cannot do myself; it is a God-dependent activity, because it is not a matter of me talking *to* God, but communicating *with* the Godhead. The Spirit translates; the Son transposes; the

Father transcends. And as I attend to prayer, keeping my ear pressed to the wall of heaven, my wrestlings find rest and I am transformed. Rarely do I walk away the same, for I have been engaged in holy communion with the Three-in-One.

A father pleading for his son once said to Jesus, "I do believe; help my unbelief" (Mark 9:24, *NASB*). It could have easily been a single mom pleading for her child—or her finances, or a relationship or her unrealized dreams. As Jesus hung on the cross, two prayers were uttered—one by Jesus (Father, forgive them, they don't know what they are doing), the other by a thief (Jesus, forgive me, I know what I've done). Jesus embodied grace, and at the cross, grace embraced the belief of a thief and the unbelief of religious zealots. Whatever category I fall into on a day-to-day basis, I am received and embraced by Grace.

Jesus continues to pray for us today. If our ears were pressed against the wall of heaven, we might hear Him praying as He did in John 17, the firstborn Son praying for His younger brothers and sisters. He prays for family unity that honors the family Name, and for an abundance of hand-me-down joy from His heart to ours. He asks for protection from our enemy, and prays for us to be constantly cleaned up from the inside out and clothed for holy purposes day by day. He prays for generations of faith that generate faith, enlarging His family. Lastly, He prays that we would experience His loving presence and ever-deepening union with the Godhead.

Today, it doesn't matter so much if my prayers are awkward and puny, or a dissonant mix of belief and unbelief, or buried too deep in my soul to find words. At the foot of the cross, I am mindful that there is One who prays for me perfectly, persistently and powerfully. His prayers wrap me in His love and enfold each day.

A PLACE OF PRAYER

My prayer is not for the world, but for those you have given me, because they belong to you. . . . I told them many things while I was with them in this world so they would be filled with my joy. . . . Make them holy by your truth;

teach them your word, which is truth. Just as you sent me into the world,
I am sending them into the world. And I give myself as a holy sacrifice
for them so they can be made holy by your truth. . . . I am praying not
only for these disciples but also for all who will ever believe in me through their
message. . . . I have revealed you to them, and I will continue to do so.
Then your love for me will be in them, and I will be in them.
JOHN 17:9,13,17-19,20,26, *NLT*

And the Holy Spirit helps us in our weakness. For example, we don't know
what God wants us to pray for. But the Holy Spirit prays for us with
groanings that cannot be expressed in words. And the Father who
knows all hearts knows what the Spirit is saying, for the Spirit pleads
for us believers in harmony with God's own will.
ROMANS 8:26-27, *NLT*

Who then will condemn us? No one—for Christ Jesus died for us
and was raised to life for us, and he is sitting in the place of honor
at God's right hand, pleading for us.
ROMANS 8:34, *NLT*

FOR REFLECTION

Just as the disciples said to Jesus, "Lord, teach us to pray," we can ask
the Holy Spirit to instruct us in prayer, aligning our hearts with His
concerns, and our minds with His point of view.

LIVING AT A PLACE NEAR HIS ALTAR

What hurdles do you face in prayer?

When you don't know how to pray or what to pray, keep it simple—
even offering God one name or one word. Let Him fill in the blanks.

Personalize Jesus' prayer in John 17 by inserting your name. How does
His prayer address current concerns in your life?

INVITING YOUR CHILDREN TO HIS ALTAR

Using Scrabble® tiles, create words representing topics for prayer (school, fear, friends, lying, and so on). Put the remaining tiles in a bowl, representing the prayers Jesus offers on your children's behalf, outside their awareness.

Be careful not to correct or amend your child's prayers—let Jesus take care of that!

Create a Family and Friends Prayer Box, using names or pictures of friends and family members from Christmas cards; add names of schoolteachers, missionaries or government leaders. Draw names each day and pray for these people.

PRAYER NOTES AND PERSONAL REFLECTIONS

WAITING

Listening to the Heartbeat of God

"Bethany, are you sure about going to Wash. U? Have you prayed about it?"

"Sure, Mom; we've prayed together at bedtime each night."

"No, that's not what I mean. I mean have *YOU* really prayed about it? Six months from now, wherever you attend college, you're going to have a *really bad day*, and wonder why you are there! Take the time to listen to God now, so you are confident of His leading."

Not only did Bethany Joy need assurance of God's leadership in her life, but I needed it too. Cutting the apron strings was becoming increasingly painful. I wasn't ready for our family to undergo yet another change. If I was sure that God had clearly led her to a far-away college, perhaps it would be a little easier to put her hand in His and let go.

Four years earlier, during my divorce, I faced the dilemma of whether or not to move across country to live near my parents and siblings. The emotional and practical support they could offer us was invaluable, but the price tag for my kids was steep—leaving school, friends and familiar surroundings. My mind chased the decision in circles; there were no easy answers. Although the court was unlikely to grant us permission, my attorney filed a petition to relocate.

For four long months, I prayed for wisdom, clarity and guidance. As I waited—on God, and on the legal process—a friend encouraged me to write down what I was "hearing" God say through the counsel of godly people who knew me well; what I was hearing through the Word; and what I was hearing in the quiet of my prayer times. As I listened, common threads and a confluence of thought emerged, confirming that moving was a good, wise decision for my family. When permission was granted, God's intervention was clear, and I moved ahead with confident assurance. I never looked back or second-guessed the decision, even in the face of difficulties.

We don't "wait" well in our fast-paced culture; we would rather go through life with a speed-pass that moves us to the front of the line, or a fast-forward button that skips commercials. Time is precious; waiting is irritating, inconvenient and unproductive. During the waiting, it can *seem* like nothing is happening—like flower bulbs germinating underground or unobservable labor contractions. But the Bible says that waiting is a worthwhile, active process of attentiveness to God that gives birth to His purposes.

The most significant changes during waiting happen *in* us, not around us. Waiting exposes attitudes to be adjusted, motives to be purified and character to be honed into the character of Christ. Waiting reveals doubts about God, nurtures faith in God and reminds us that we are not in control; God is. Waiting creates space in our lives to listen attentively to the Spirit of God, and painfully pries our personal agendas out of our fingers so that we can grasp God's agenda. "Wait for the Lord," a repetitive refrain in the book of Psalms, is often paired with words that tell us what to do while we wait: seek, watch, listen, trust, hope. Waiting gives us an opportunity to press into God's unfailing love and watch His unfolding plan, resulting in our worship and thanksgiving.

At the foot of the cross, we remember that Jesus was the long-awaited Messiah, the "Coming One." During centuries of anticipation, some got tired of waiting and pursued other gods. Others were distracted and chased their own agendas. Still others got careless in waiting, forgetting to watch and failing to recognize His arrival. But God revealed the Messiah to those who waited attentively.

Two thousand years later, we wait for the return of the "Coming One." Our waiting is not passive, but purposeful—He's left work for us to do! Like our forebears, we are also easily tired, distracted or careless. But if we are attentive, we recognize the ways He comes to us in the daily circumstances of our lives, and we watch His larger purposes unfold.

After a day of fasting and prayer, Bethany Joy changed her college decision, choosing a college she had applied to very reluctantly. God honored her desire to listen to Him and gave her clarity in her decision-making process. She's never looked back; the school was a perfect fit for her. It was still hard to let her go, but I smiled in my tears, knowing that she was walking with her Father.

A PLACE OF PRAYER

I wait for you, O Lord; you will answer, O Lord my God.
PSALM 38:15

I wait for the LORD, my soul waits, and in his word I put my hope.
My soul waits for the Lord more than watchmen wait for the morning,
more than watchmen wait for the morning.
PSALM 130:5-6

I say to myself, "The LORD is my portion; therefore I will wait for him."
The LORD is good to those whose hope is in him, to the one who seeks him;
it is good to wait quietly for the salvation of the LORD.
LAMENTATIONS 3:24-26

I will climb up to my watch tower and stand at my guardpost. There I will
wait to see what the LORD says and how he will answer my complaint.
HABAKKUK 2:1, *NLT*

Now you have every spiritual gift you need as you eagerly wait for
the return of our Lord Jesus Christ.
1 CORINTHIANS 1:7, *NLT*

FOR REFLECTION

Just as the night watchman waits confidently for morning, we can wait on God with quiet anticipation.

LIVING AT A PLACE NEAR HIS ALTAR

When is waiting most difficult for you?

Can you recall a time when you were glad you waited, rather than rushing ahead?

Do you need to listen to the Lord concerning a current decision in your life? What does He want you to do while you wait for His answer?

INVITING YOUR CHILDREN TO HIS ALTAR

Play Mother, May I? to demonstrate the importance of asking and attentive listening.

Can your children recall a time when it was difficult to wait for something important? Was there any benefit in waiting? What did they learn about themselves in the process? Discuss character traits that are developed through waiting.

When your child faces a decision, use this helpful acronym, "**WAIT**," to weigh it out: **W**atch (observe circumstances); **A**sk (seek guidance from God and wise people); **I**nvestigate (find out the facts); **T**alk (to people who know you well and love you).

PRAYER NOTES AND PERSONAL REFLECTIONS

FELLOWSHIP

Partnering with God

When my husband and I separated after 20 years of marriage, I didn't have a clue how to do life on my own, but I knew someone who did: Mary Anne. Mary Anne was a godly, 80-year-young whippersnapper who had never married. Beneath her unassuming demeanor, Mary Anne was rock-solid in her convictions and solid gold in her character. She approached life pragmatically—pressing it through the filter of God's Word, calling a spade a spade. Her mind was sharp and her heart discerning. At Bible study, I constantly scooped up pearls of wisdom that spilled from her lips. Mary Anne loved life and loved people, and she enjoyed a wide web of relationships—but she was also fiercely independent. If anyone could teach me how to live fully and successfully as a single woman, it was Mary Anne. I wasted no time asking if she would mentor me.

Every Tuesday afternoon, Mary Anne and I sipped coffee at my dining room table, sorting out the cards I had been dealt that week. Her knobby fingers matter-of-factly pointed out the heart of a matter by identifying what mattered to God's heart. Mary Anne knew God's heart because He had been her life partner for over 60 years. She had running conversations with God throughout her day—muttering to Him while she drove, talking out loud as she worked in her kitchen and chatting with Him about Scriptures she read each day in her favorite blue recliner. She asked Him questions and listened for His answers. She faithfully prayed for others, knowing that Jesus was her intercessory prayer partner at the Throne of Grace.

The most important lessons I learned from Mary Anne weren't about being a single woman, but about enjoying partnership with

God by living all the moments of the day in prayer. I learned that the extraordinary woman I perceived as *independent* was actually very *dependent*—on God. Paul said to pray without ceasing (see 1 Thessalonians 5:17), and that's how Mary Anne did life.

I consider Mary Anne a modern-day saint who followed in the footsteps of Enoch, Noah and Abraham. In the midst of a long genealogy, the Bible tells us that Enoch "walked with God 300 years" (Genesis 5:22,24). The *NIV* text note points out this phrase in contrast to the six individuals in previous generations who "lived" a certain number of years, then died. Some "live," others "walk with God," a relationship rooted in faith. Hebrews 11, cataloging people of faith, reminds us that Noah also "walked with God"; when he heard the rain hitting the roof of the ark, he was glad he had listened and obeyed! Abraham walked with God far out on a limb—leaving his homeland with no clear destination, because God said, "Get up and go." *Left, right, left, right, listen, obey, listen, obey.*

These ancient people of faith were familiar with God's voice because He was their walking companion. I imagine they enjoyed running conversations with Him similar to the ongoing conversations I have with my current walking partner. Mary Kay and I hash over the daily stuff of life, pick each other's brains and mull over problems—all the while enjoying each other's company. Just like Mary Anne and God.

Jesus had this kind of partnership with God. He snuck away early in the morning and stayed up late just to get time alone with Him. Jesus constantly listened to His Father, doing what the Father prompted Him to do, and speaking the words He heard the Father speaking. He promised that we, too, could become familiar with the Father's voice and enjoy His companionship. "My sheep listen to my voice; I know them, and they follow me" (John 10:27). According to Jesus, this kind of relational intimacy with the Godhead is the norm for His followers—it is the fellowship that He came to restore through His death on the cross. Through faith in Jesus and what He did for us on the cross, we are adopted into the family of God and invited to join the family circle of conversation that runs behind the scenes in the heavenlies, yet transcends our daily lives.

Mary Anne moved to her heavenly home a few years ago, where she continues to partner with God more fully than ever. My conversations with her have been suspended, but I assume that her running conversations with God haven't missed a beat. As I chat with God at my kitchen sink, I notice Mary Anne's picture on my window sill and thank God that instead of teaching me how to live as a "fiercely independent" single woman, Mary Anne showed me how to live in a tenaciously dependent partnership with God through prayer.

A PLACE OF PRAYER

*Serve only the Lord your God and fear him alone. Obey his commands,
listen to his voice, and cling to him.*
DEUTERONOMY 13:4, *NLT*

*Now He [Jesus] was telling them a parable to show that at all times
they ought to pray and not to lose heart.*
LUKE 18:1, *NASB*

My sheep listen to my voice; I know them, and they follow me.
JOHN 10:27, *NLT*

*Pray in the Spirit at all times and on every occasion. Stay alert
and be persistent in your prayers for all believers everywhere.*
EPHESIANS 6:18, *NLT*

*We saw it, we heard it, and now we're telling you so you can
experience it along with us, this experience of communion with the Father
and his Son, Jesus Christ. Our motive for writing is simply this:
We want you to enjoy this, too. Your joy will double our joy!*
1 JOHN 1:3-4, *THE MESSAGE*

FOR REFLECTION

Through the course of a day, our prayers might vary, but all are expressions of our dependence on God.

LIVING AT A PLACE NEAR HIS ALTAR

What are your usual topics of conversation with God? Are there topics you avoid?

When and where do you usually pray? Set an alarm on your cell phone to remind you to pray at intervals throughout your day.

How does the concept of partnering with God change your view of prayer?

INVITING YOUR CHILDREN TO HIS ALTAR

Let your children eavesdrop as you converse with God about daily events or concerns.

Talk often about answers to prayer so your children will recognize God's involvement in daily life.

Model partnering with God by praying with your children in the moment of their struggles; for example, anxiety over a math test, difficulty with a classmate or a disappointment in sports.

PRAYER NOTES AND PERSONAL REFLECTIONS

_____
_____
_____
_____
_____
_____
_____
_____
_____
_____
_____
_____

DAY 22

PRIDE

Dying to Reputation

Our marital separation provided grist for the church rumor mill. Like gapers who slow down when passing an accident on the freeway, people shook their heads, assessed the twisted fragments of our wreckage and devised theories about the demise of our marriage. The assumptions and presumptions formed out of ignorance and based on half-truths, or no truth at all, caught me off guard, adding insult to injury. But I was powerless to do anything about it. I couldn't afford to waste my energy trying to control or change that reality. After spending years finding freedom from internally shaming messages, I had no desire to be enslaved again. *What will people think?* I couldn't let that matter. People would think whatever they wanted to think. I had to bite my tongue and let it go. *So this is what it means to die to reputation.*

I was also unprepared for the shift in relationships. My closest friends remained solid sources of emotional support in my life. But others turned aloof; plastic smiles masked emotional distancing, disappointment and disapproval. I felt hurt, but also felt sympathy. I had stood in their shoes and made similar arms-length judgments over the years when other couples separated. Our human tendency to righteously evaluate other people's lives is insidious; pride is one-size-fits-all. God used the judgments of others to help me see my own prideful attitudes.

Two truths became clear to me: You don't know someone's story unless they have told it to you. And if you've never walked in their moccasins, then you don't really know what you would do in their situation. Every time I felt foolishly judged by others, I found myself repenting for times I had ignorantly done the same in the past. *Father, forgive them; they don't know what they are doing.*

We expend a lot of energy earning, maintaining and protecting our reputation. But we can easily get off the mark when motivated by pride. Self-justification, self-defense, self-righteousness, self-absorption—we become wrapped up in a lot of "self."

As a Jew, the apostle Paul had a sterling reputation: "I was circumcised when I was eight days old. I am a pure-blooded citizen of Israel and a member of the tribe of Benjamin—a real Hebrew if there ever was one! I was a member of the Pharisees, who demand the strictest obedience to the Jewish law. I was so zealous that I harshly persecuted the church. And as for righteousness, I obeyed the law without fault." (Philippians 3:5-6, *NLT*). But after his conversion to Christ, Paul viewed his reputation differently. "I once thought these things were valuable, but now I consider them worthless because of what Christ has done. Yes, everything else is worthless when compared with the infinite value of knowing Christ Jesus my Lord. For his sake I have discarded everything else, *counting it all as garbage, so that I could gain Christ and become one with him*" (Philippians 3:7-9, *NLT*, emphasis added). Paul exchanged the self-life for the Christ-life; the only name that mattered now, the only name he defended, was Christ's name. Finding his identity in Christ alone, Paul aligned himself with Christ in every way, even "to know . . . the fellowship of sharing in his sufferings" (v. 10).

We readily recognize Christ's suffering on the cross, but His sufferings were not only physical. What was it like for the King of kings and Lord of lords to be sized up by the prideful people He created? The Holy One endured the ridicule of the religious elite for socializing with "sinners." During His trial, the Righteous One chose the suffering of silence rather than justifying or defending Himself before His accusers. What kind of humility enabled the One who is all-wise and all-knowing to tolerate being tested, judged and misunderstood?

In life and in death, humility characterized Jesus, "who, being in very nature God, did not consider equality with God something to be grasped, but made himself nothing, taking the very nature of a servant, being made in human likeness. And being found in appearance as a man, he humbled himself and became obedient to death—even death on a cross!" (Philippians 2:6-8).

Perhaps my experiences of being misunderstood, wrongly judged, sized up and scrutinized were in some small way a taste of the "fellowship of His sufferings." Certainly, God used them to etch some humility in me. Dying to reputation helped me remember that it's not about me—never has been, never will be. It's all about Him, from beginning to end. When I get that right, that's all that matters.

A PLACE OF HUMILITY

When pride comes, then comes dishonor, but with the humble is wisdom.
PROVERBS 11:2, *NASB*

The high and lofty one who lives in eternity, the Holy One, says this: "I live in the high and holy place with those whose spirits are contrite and humble. I restore the crushed spirit of the humble and revive the courage of those with repentant hearts."
ISAIAH 57:15, *NLT*

Your attitude should be the same as that of Christ Jesus: Who, being in very nature God, did not consider equality with God something to be grasped, but made himself nothing, taking the very nature of a servant, being made in human likeness. And being found in appearance as a man, he humbled himself and became obedient to death—even death on a cross! Therefore God exalted him to the highest place and gave him the name that is above every name, that at the name of Jesus every knee should bow, in heaven and on earth and under the earth, and every tongue confess that Jesus Christ is Lord, to the glory of God the Father.
PHILIPPIANS 2:5-11

FOR REFLECTION

If I am concerned about anyone's reputation, let it be the reputation of Christ in me. That reputation is built on humility and love.

LIVING AT A PLACE NEAR HIS ALTAR

When have you felt judged by others? How have you judged others in the same way?

When are you tempted to defend your reputation?

Do you have a reputation built on humility and love?

INVITING YOUR CHILDREN TO HIS ALTAR

When have your children been worried about their reputation? Have they ever judged or hurt the reputation of others?

Read several definitions of humility and pride; discuss the difference between a reputation built on godly character and one based on pride.

Ask your children to identify some ways that Jesus demonstrated humility during His betrayal, trial and crucifixion (see Matthew 26–27).

PRAYER NOTES AND PERSONAL REFLECTIONS

INADEQUACY

The Comparison Trap

The parent orientation at the beginning of each school year is a bit daunting to me. My mind spins with dates to remember, volumes of Very Important Papers to read and too many meetings to attend. Pep talks to "get involved" are followed by tables layered with enough sign-up sheets to wallpaper my bathroom. I mentally brace myself to withstand both the internal and external pressure to *do one more thing* by determining beforehand how many and what kinds of commitments I can realistically manage. As a single parent, I sometimes feel inadequate; there's just not quite enough of me to go around.

Inadequate. That's what the 12 disciples felt as their eyes scanned the sea of faces. Over 5,000 people had followed them to this remote place, and Jesus had been teaching into the evening (see Mark 6:30-42; John 6:1-13). Everyone was tired and hungry. Jesus' disciples saw the overwhelming need and came to Jesus empty-handed. *Send them away, Jesus. We don't have enough to feed all these people.* Did Jesus have a twinkle in His eye and a smile at the corner of His mouth when He asked, *How much do you have?* Was Andrew sarcastic when he pointed out that a little boy's lunch of bread and fish was inadequate to feed that many faces?

But the little boy gave his sack lunch to Jesus: five loaves and two fishes. Perhaps it was just a simple expression of gratefulness and love for Jesus. But Jesus took the lunch, gave thanks to God and started passing it out—I imagine with great hilarity! Surely it wasn't in the child's wildest dreams that Jesus would feed the whole crowd with his lunch! But He did; in Jesus' hands, the bread and fish became more than enough. There were even leftovers!

I often identify with that little boy. I'm brown-bagging it through life—toting my bundle of limited resources of time, energy, gifts and abilities. As I observe the capabilities of other women and admire their accomplishments, I feel like a little tugboat chugging along next to freighters, cruise ships and aircraft carriers. Comparison consistently breeds a sense of inadequacy. But figuring out what kind of "boat" I was designed to be, and respecting my lading level (the weight limit a vessel can carry before sinking), has been extremely liberating—helping me honor God's design and purposes for me, honor my own gifts and abilities and honor others without envying them or diminishing myself. An attitude of true humility is not demonstrated in self-deprecation but in honestly assessing strengths and limitations and giving them over to God.

At the foot of the cross there is no room for comparison, only comparing ourselves to God's holy standard. From God's point of view, *all* "fall short of the glory of God" (Romans 3:23). On the cross, Jesus covered all our shortcomings and inadequacies. Those who trust in Him, He *fully* equips and empowers for His good purposes through His Holy Spirit. My adequacy is in Him and through Him, from start to finish. It's not what I do for Him; it's what He does through me!

All I've got is my little sack lunch; all Jesus wants is for me to give it to Him in faith and out of love. When I do, He delights in using it in surprising ways, for His glory!

A PLACE OF HUMILITY

*The only accurate way to understand ourselves is by what God is
and by what he does for us, not by what we are and what we do for him.
In this way we are like the various parts of a human body. Each part
gets its meaning from the body as a whole, not the other way around.
The body we're talking about is Christ's body of chosen people. Each of us
finds our meaning and function as a part of his body. But as a chopped-off
finger or cut-off toe we wouldn't amount to much, would we? So since
we find ourselves fashioned into all these excellently formed and marvelously
functioning parts in Christ's body, let's just go ahead and be what we*

were made to be, without enviously or pridefully comparing ourselves
with each other, or trying to be something we aren't.
ROMANS 12:3-5, *THE MESSAGE*

If the whole body were an eye, how would you hear? Or if your
whole body were an ear, how would you smell anything? But our bodies
have many parts, and God has put each part just where he wants it. . . .
The eye can never say to the hand, "I don't need you." The head can't say
to the feet, "I don't need you." In fact, some parts of the body that seem
weakest and least important are actually the most necessary.
1 CORINTHIANS 12:17-18,21-22, *NLT*

Not that we are adequate in ourselves to consider anything as coming
from ourselves, but our adequacy is from God.
2 CORINTHIANS 3:5, *NASB*

Now may the God of peace . . . equip you with all you need for doing his will.
May he produce in you, through the power of Jesus Christ, every good thing that
is pleasing to him. All glory to him forever and ever! Amen.
HEBREWS 13:20-21, *NLT*

FOR REFLECTION

I am custom-designed by God: a unique mixture of aptitudes and
affinities, experiences and expertise, passions and priorities—all useful
in big and small ways for His purposes.

LIVING AT A PLACE NEAR HIS ALTAR

How does comparison feed your sense of inadequacy?

What type of "vessel" are you, and what is your "lading level"?

Make a list of your aptitudes, experiences, passions and talents. Ask
God to reveal creative ways He can use them for His purposes.

INVITING YOUR CHILDREN TO HIS ALTAR

Using permanent markers, write some of the positive qualities of each family member on inexpensive vinyl placemats. Let everyone contribute by writing in his or her own hand on one another's placemats and decorating his or her own mats. Thank God together for each child's unique design.

Look for positive qualities to verbally affirm in your child. Avoid comparison, such as "Why can't you be like . . . ?" To compare is to diminish your child's unique design.

Consider how your child's strengths can be developed to serve others: a teenager who likes children could serve in a Sunday School class or at a summer camp; a creative elementary-age child could design the family Christmas card or make Christmas decorations for a local retirement home.

PRAYER NOTES AND PERSONAL REFLECTIONS

FACING LIMITATIONS

I Can't, but God Can

My high school violin instructor's bow flashed over the strings as her fingers deftly danced on the fingerboard of the violin; she made it look so easy!

"Now you try it," she said, and my inevitable reply was "I can't."

"Don't say 'I can't', say 'I'll try,'" she chided.

We had this dialogue on a regular basis, more times than I can count. "Can't" was a four-letter word not to be uttered in her studio; everyone could *try*. Of course, what I meant was that I couldn't reproduce her sound or match her technique; in short, I couldn't play like she did—not even close, not even in a million years. I wasn't sure if the scratchy notes I produced would even marginally resemble music. Violin lessons were regular and occasionally humiliating reminders of my limitations.

I vividly remember sitting on my porch one afternoon shortly after my husband and I separated. I had always wanted to be a mom, but I had never wanted to be a *single* mom. Parenting was the most challenging, most satisfying and most important job I would ever have, but I didn't sign up to do it alone! As the future loomed ahead of me, the prospect of parenting alone was nothing less than terrifying. How would I manage? How could I possibly ever handle all the responsibilities before me? How could I ever be "enough" for my children? Just as surely as I had a realistic estimation of myself as a violinist, I also had a realistic estimation of myself as a parent. *I can't. I can't do it all; I can't do it alone; I can't meet all the needs; I can't bear the load; I can't be enough. I CAN'T DO THIS!*

What I lacked in that moment was a realistic estimation of God. For every "I can't" in our lexicon, God has an "I can." He brings us to the end of ourselves—face to face with our limitations—to bring us to Himself, face to face with His unlimited power. Jesus said it simply: "Apart from me you can do nothing" (John 15:5). He saw my complete inadequacy in starker terms than I like to admit on a daily basis. But Jesus also said, "The person who trusts me will not only do what I'm doing but even greater things, because I, on my way to the Father, am giving you the same work to do that I've been doing. You can count on it. From now on, whatever you request along the lines of who I am and what I am doing, I'll do it. That's how the Father will be seen for who he is in the Son. I mean it. Whatever you request in this way, I'll do" (John 14:12, *THE MESSAGE*). His message is clear: *You can't, but I can.*

The cross of Christ is the most poignant "you can't, but I can" summary statement God ever made. From the beginning of time, all our best efforts at trying to be "good enough" have fallen short of God's mark; God saw that we were powerless and took it upon Himself to be the remedy. On the cross, Jesus offered Himself as the only adequate One, bringing our merit-based efforts to gain eternal life to a screeching halt. Just as He remedied our inability to earn eternal life, He meets us in our limitations in daily life. His marvelous plan was to come live within us, filling us with His power for any and every situation. The secret of daily empowerment is to actually give up self-effort; the secret of daily empowerment is the humility of dependence. *I can't, but He can.*

A PLACE OF HUMILITY

Yes, I am the vine; you are the branches.
Those who remain in me, and I in them, will produce much fruit.
For apart from me you can do nothing.
JOHN 15:5, *NLT*

Such confidence as this is ours through Christ before God. Not that we
are competent in ourselves to claim anything for ourselves,
but our competence comes from God.
2 CORINTHIANS 3:4-5

"My grace is all you need. My power works best in weakness." So now I am glad to boast about my weaknesses, so that the power of Christ can work through me. That's why I take pleasure in my weaknesses, and in the insults, hardships, persecutions, and troubles that I suffer for Christ. For when I am weak, then I am strong.
2 CORINTHIANS 12:9-10, *NLT*

For I can do everything through Christ, who gives me strength.
PHILIPPIANS 4:13

For God did not give us a spirit of timidity, but a spirit of power, of love and of self-discipline.
2 TIMOTHY 1:7

FOR REFLECTION

I can't.

BUT I CAN.

I can't do it all.

I CAN DO IT ALL.

I can't do it alone.

YOU ARE NOT ALONE; I AM WITH YOU.

I WILL BE IN YOU AND DO IT THROUGH YOU.

I can't ever meet all my kids' needs.

YOU CAN'T, BUT I CAN.

I can't bear the load.

I DID, AND I CAN. LET ME CARRY IT.

I can't be enough.

YOU NEVER WERE. I AM ENOUGH.

I CAN'T DO THIS!

I AGREE. BUT TOGETHER, WE CAN.

LIVING AT A PLACE NEAR HIS ALTAR

When do you say, "I can't"? What is God's "I can" response to you?

What are your strengths and weaknesses as a parent?

Lean into God; ask Him to empower your strengths and equip you in your areas of weakness beyond your natural ability.

INVITING YOUR CHILDREN TO HIS ALTAR

When your children say, "I can't," challenge them to say, "I'll try." Encourage them to ask God for help. Give them room to do things imperfectly, and affirm their efforts.

What do your children consider their strengths and weaknesses? How could God use your child's unique set of strengths and weaknesses for good? Encourage your child to humbly give both to God. Thank God together for your child's unique design.

Take a walk in your neighborhood and notice the flowering or fruit trees. Explain how the branches are nourished by water from the roots, producing fruit. What happens to the flower or fruit if the branch is cut off from the tree? Relate this to Jesus' illustration in John 15:5 of our dependence on Him.

PRAYER NOTES AND PERSONAL REFLECTIONS

_____

_____

_____

_____

_____

_____

_____

_____

_____

INJUSTICE

The Unfairness of God's Grace

"But that's not fair!" my daughter retorted as she stomped away. No one has to teach children that line; it readily rolls off their little tongues faster than you can say "Time out!" She and her sister silently scowled and stewed for the next five minutes in their respective "time-out chairs" in opposite corners of the most boring room of our house, the dining room.

Children have a deeply embedded sense of fairness; they know instinctively when the scales are tipped. Injustice provides fertile ground for roots of bitterness and resentment to grow, squelching any willingness to forgive. If the scales are constantly tipped against them, children give up thinking fairness is ever a reasonable expectation. If the scales are consistently tipped in their favor, children gain a sense of entitlement. The former spoils hope and breeds discouragement; the latter spoils humility and fosters pride.

We all want a fair shake in life. Most single moms I know experience the rub of injustice in their personal circumstances—usually financially, often professionally and sometimes socially. And we always feel it for our kids. I'm keenly aware of all that is less-than-fair in my children's world—hurts they did not deserve and losses they have had to assimilate that I can never "make right" for them. Whether propelled by sadness, anger or guilt, we often overcompensate, wearing ourselves out in our attempts to create fairness for our children in every arena we can. But when we make "fair" the rule of thumb, we can do our children a disservice. Demonstrating God's justice, we can fail to demonstrate His other attributes.

While justice is an important value to strive for and instill in our children, it doesn't get the last word. Love does. Our heavenly Father showed us that truth in Jesus. Jesus never taught that "fair" was the rule that settled the score in life or in relationships. He always taught the rule of love. Sometimes, love is demonstrated through fairness. But God's sense of fairness, mitigated by love, does not always look the way we expect. Jesus said the rain falls on the righteous and the un-righteous—is that fair or not? In the parable of the hired workers (see Matthew 20:1-16), the landowner paid each worker the agreed wages—which was the same amount for those hired in the last hour as for those who had worked all day. Was that fair or not?

If God's only standard was "fair," we would all lose. Because of sin, we would get exactly what we deserve: judgment. But God saw that the scales were hopelessly tipped against us; on the cross, He made right what we were helpless to ever make right ourselves. God's righteousness, justice, love and mercy perfectly intersected on the beams of the cross. His sacrifice provided atonement. His mercy gave us hope. His grace gives us humility.

Forgiveness exceeds fairness; God's love trumps all. When we fall short, His love offers us mercy—not doling out the judgment we de-serve. When we don't measure up, His love grants us grace—offering us what we don't deserve: salvation, new life in Christ, the indwelling Holy Spirit and all the promises of God. In the end, on the receiving end, grace and mercy are what we really want—more than we want life to be fair. Our disappointment that life isn't fair is superseded by the discovery and relief that life in Christ is based on the rule of love.

After my daughters finished their "time out," they joined me on the big green couch in our living room. We identified their point of contention and discussed what resolution would seem "fair" to each of them. But the final question was, "What would be the loving thing to do?" Love chose to forgive the offense; love always gets the last word.

A PLACE OF FORGIVENESS

He has showed you, O man, what is good. And what does the Lord require of
you? To act justly and to love mercy and to walk humbly with your God.
MICAH 6:8

Therefore, since we have been made right in God's sight by faith,
we have peace with God because of what Jesus Christ our Lord has done for us.
Because of our faith, Christ has brought us into this place of undeserved
privilege where we now stand, and we confidently and joyfully look
forward to sharing God's glory. . . . When we were utterly helpless,
Christ came at just the right time and died for us sinners. Now,
most people would not be willing to die for an upright person, though
someone might perhaps be willing to die for a person who is especially good.
But God showed his great love for us by sending Christ to die for us
while we were still sinners.
ROMANS 5:1-2,6-8, *NLT*

You have come to Jesus, the one who mediates the new covenant between
God and people, and to the sprinkled blood, which speaks of forgiveness
instead of crying out for vengeance like the blood of Abel.
HEBREWS 12:24, *NLT*

Talk and act like a person expecting to be judged by the Rule that sets us free.
For if you refuse to act kindly, you can hardly expect to be treated kindly.
Kind mercy wins over harsh judgment every time.
JAMES 2:12-13, *THE MESSAGE*

FOR REFLECTION

On the cross, grace and mercy settled the score, and love got the last word. This is the kind of forgiveness God offers us and calls us to offer others.

LIVING AT A PLACE NEAR HIS ALTAR

What seems unfair in your life today? What would your life look like if it was "fair"?

How has bitterness or resentment over injustice strangled your ability to forgive someone?

How have you benefited from the unfairness of God's grace and mercy?

INVITING YOUR CHILDREN TO HIS ALTAR

Ask your child to cut the next pizza or batch of brownies; let everyone else choose their pieces first. Did the outcome seem fair? Why, or why not?

What is a situation that seems unfair to your child? What would be a fair solution? What would be the loving solution?

Use two intersecting Popsicle sticks to make a cross. On the horizontal crossbar, write "righteousness" and "justice." On the vertical stick, write "love" and "mercy." Read definitions of these words from a dictionary; explain how Jesus satisfied the requirements of righteousness, justice, love and mercy through His death on the cross.

PRAYER NOTES AND PERSONAL REFLECTIONS

FREEDOM FROM GUILT

The Ground Is Level at the Foot of the Cross

While growing up in a Christian home, I was a pretty good kid who "played by the rules." Later, as a wife, I conscientiously studied the Bible, read books, attended seminars and sought mentors to learn how to be a "Christian wife." Years later, in the shattering pain of marital separation, I could identify ways that I had been wronged, but I had difficulty seeing my contribution to the outcome of our relationship. Hadn't I "played by the rules" to the best of my ability?

As I licked my wounds, the prospect of forgiving my husband loomed in front of me like a mountain I could not scale. The infractions seemed too great, my wounds too deep; I felt overwhelmed by the impossible. Contrary to our culture of quick fixes, there are no shortcuts to forgiveness. Rather, forgiveness is a long, arduous journey, one we do not feel ready for right away and, in truth, cannot accomplish until we have faced our pain head-on—the pain inflicted by the other and our own painful part in the messy outcome. Neither is easy to address, but both have the power to keep us shackled in invisible bondage to our most insidious enemy, pride. Our uncanny ability to keep a lengthy laundry list of another's violations actually enables us to avoid recognizing our own shortcomings and failures. We rationalize weaknesses we cannot avoid seeing. Self-righteousness preempts humility.

During that time of separation, I began to pray through the chapters of *The Power of a Praying Wife* by Stormie O'Martian. I hoped that God would use this focused time in daily prayer to change the outcome of our marriage. God had other plans; He used it to change my perspective. As I prayed for my husband, I began to see myself from a different vantage point. God exposed my own black bundle of shortcomings, weaknesses and foibles and their impact on my husband over the years, exposing my own very deep need for grace. At the foot of the cross, I identified and grieved the ways that my relationship with my husband had been surreptitiously undermined by attitudes and choices rooted in my hidden pride and self-centeredness. God had seen it all along, but I had not. As I faced the ugly mess, my loving Father gathered me into His arms, whispering words of love, grace and mercy that He had waited so long to offer me. Later, I penned a letter to my husband, owning my part and asking his forgiveness. Weighing and laying blame gave way to taking responsibility, no matter how little or large.

Experiencing God's forgiveness is a vital prerequisite for the ongoing process of extending forgiveness, grace and mercy toward others. Seeing my own brokenness, my "un-whole-ness," enables me to see another's weaknesses and struggles through the lens of compassion and continually frees me from the traps of resentment, bitterness, and self-pity. Forgiveness doesn't mean wrongs are of no consequence; it means the consequences of sin were so severe that only Jesus could pay the penalty of sin. At the altar of the cross, God's generous grace trumped justice, and I am the beneficiary of His mercy. If a holy God could forgive me, then who am I not to forgive another who also stands in need of grace? Forgiveness means humbly acknowledging that the ground is level at the foot of the cross.

A PLACE OF FORGIVENESS

Lord, if you kept a record of our sins, who, O Lord, could ever survive?
But you offer forgiveness, that we might learn to fear you.
PSALM 130:3-4, *NLT*

"I tell you, her sins—and they are many—have been forgiven, so she has
shown me much love. But a person who is forgiven little shows only little love."
Then Jesus said to the woman, "Your sins are forgiven."
LUKE 7:47-48, *NLT*

Instead, be kind to each other, tenderhearted, forgiving one another,
just as God through Christ has forgiven you.
EPHESIANS 4:32, *NLT*

He canceled the record of the charges against us and took it away
by nailing it to the cross.
COLOSSIANS 2:14, *NLT*

Make allowance for each other's faults, and forgive anyone who offends you.
Remember, the Lord forgave you, so you must forgive others.
COLOSSIANS 3:13, *NLT*

If we claim we have no sin, we are only fooling ourselves and not living in the
truth. But if we confess our sins to him, he is faithful and just to forgive us our sins
and to cleanse us from all wickedness. If we claim we have not sinned, we are
calling God a liar and showing that his word has no place in our hearts.
1 JOHN 1:8-10, *NLT*

FOR REFLECTION

In the midst of His pain, Jesus hung on the cross and said, "Father, forgive them, they do not know what they are doing." Allow His forgiveness to create channels of grace in you that overflow toward others.

LIVING AT A PLACE NEAR HIS ALTAR

Keep short accounts with God and others. Ask Him to reveal attitudes of selfishness and pride that lead to choices that grieve Him. Seek His forgiveness and the forgiveness of others as He exposes areas of sin.

When you are wounded by another, do you nurse the wound with self-righteous pride and self-pity? Instead, choose to live in forgiveness by returning to the foot of the cross and remembering the grace given you. Let go of the pain as you choose to let God faithfully deal with your offender.

Who do you need to forgive today?

INVITING YOUR CHILDREN TO HIS ALTAR

When dealing with sibling squabbling, give your children a time out to consider their part in the conflict. Instead of letting them point fingers at each other, ask each one to own what they said or did that was not loving or kind, consider what they could have done differently, offer apologies and seek forgiveness. Help them practice the humility of taking responsibility for their contribution to the problem. This discipline not only enables them to experience the reality that unresolved conflict creates separation in relationships, but it also helps them learn skills of conflict resolution and protects their ongoing relationship from resentment and bitterness.

Remind your children that love is the rule in relationships, not "fairness." Point out that God's love goes beyond what is fair, expressing itself in grace and mercy toward us.

PRAYER NOTES AND PERSONAL REFLECTIONS

FORGIVING THE UNFORGIVABLE

The Unreasonable Grace of God

Lots of "stuff" happens to us at the hands of other people. When we have been wounded in some fashion, each rung up the ladder of wrongs requires a bit more of us to move past it and move on with our lives. The not-so-bad stuff is annoying, like tripping over a stone in the path. We recover our footing and keep going, often without a backward glance. As they say, don't sweat the small stuff. At the far opposite end of the spectrum are the wounds that slice us to the core and leave us gasping for air, mouthing incomplete sentences. The pain is both excruciating and numbing. Years later, just thinking of these violations, our knees wobble and our stomachs turn. Sometimes, we subconsciously lock the monster of pain in the deep freeze of our souls; if we let it out, it might eat us alive. Like a boulder wedged in a mountain pass, these wounds are incomprehensible and impassable.

This is the mystery and the dilemma: If you can't wrap your mind around the wound, how can you possibly forgive it? If you can't forgive it, how can you ever move past it?

During my marital separation, I struggled deeply with the issue of forgiving wrongs I deemed unforgivable. Sometimes, the struggle merely consisted of my determination to keep the issue of forgiveness at arm's length. Eventually, I reached the unavoidable boulder in the road; I had to move past it in order to move on in my own healing and growth. As long as I tolerated an unforgiving spirit in myself, I was stuck—held hostage to the pain of my wounds. My heart was in danger of becoming as hard as that boulder. I realized I did not want to continue to give another person or my painful past that kind of power in my life.

But this was the catch: to move the boulder in the road, I needed off-the-charts amounts of grace and mercy, and I just didn't have it in me; my well had run dry. It all came to a head one quiet evening alone in an upstairs bedroom, where I was in a profound wrestling match with God. I desperately wanted the freedom that forgiveness would bring to my own soul, but I was so utterly bankrupt—in my estimation, the debt was too great to forgive, the wounds too deep, the violations too outrageous. How could I let it all go? I finally came whimpering to the foot of the cross—broken, depleted and empty. Sobbing, I blurted out loud to God, *"I CAN'T."*

And that is when the wrestling match ended. God lifted me off the wrestling mat and cradled me in His loving arms. He said, *I know you can't. But I can. That is why I hung on the cross. You cannot forgive the debt of pain any more than another can ever repay it. Forgiving will never mean either of you settled the debt. It will always mean that I settled the debt, once and for all, on the cross. Let Me forgive through you; let "Christ in you, the hope of glory" do the thing you cannot ever reasonably, sensibly do in the flesh. Let Me live in you and through you."*

In my utter powerlessness, Jesus Christ became utterly powerful. He unleashed His unreasonable grace, both toward me in my impoverished spirit, and through me toward my ex-husband. I merely became His cooperative conduit. In the process, I was released from the bondage of an unforgiving spirit and from the pain of my wounds. *I* was the one who was let go!

That experience proved to be a catalyst in my relationship with Christ and in my journey toward healing. Living in forgiveness is not about mustering up massive good will toward another, but positioning myself at the foot of the cross to be both a recipient and channel of God's extravagant grace. That experience also enabled me to coach my children as they grappled with forgiveness, showing them how to live out truly amazing, off-the-charts grace—because it is completely from the Spirit. This is the real mystery: "Christ in you, the hope of glory" (Colossians 1:27).

A PLACE OF FORGIVENESS

*He does not punish us for all our sins; he does not deal harshly with us, as we
deserve . . . He has removed our sins as far from us as the east is from the west.
The Lord is like a father to his children, tender and compassionate to those who
fear him. For he knows how weak we are; he remembers we are only dust.*
PSALM 103:10,12-14, *NLT*

*Then Peter came to him and asked, "Lord, how often should I
forgive someone who sins against me? Seven times?"
"No, not seven times," Jesus replied, "but seventy times seven!"*
MATTHEW 18:21-22, *NLT*

*Each time he said, "My grace is all you need. My power works best
in weakness." So now I am glad to boast about my weaknesses, so that
the power of Christ can work through me.*
2 CORINTHIANS 12:9, *NLT*

*May you experience the love of Christ, though it is too great to understand fully.
Then you will be made complete with all the fullness of life and power that comes
from God. Now all glory to God, who is able, through his mighty power at work
within us, to accomplish infinitely more than we might ask or think.*
EPHESIANS 3:19-20, *NLT*

FOR REFLECTION

Living in forgiveness is the ongoing process of humbly circling the foot
of the cross and allowing the living Christ *in* me to live *through* me. As
we come to Him empty-handed, He is faithful to fill and empower us.

LIVING AT A PLACE NEAR HIS ALTAR

What wounds in your life do you deem unforgivable?
What keeps you from forgiving the one who wounded you?
How has unforgiveness blocked your path toward healing?

INVITING YOUR CHILDREN TO HIS ALTAR

Cultivate humility in your children by establishing patterns of asking for and extending forgiveness in the family circle.

Ask your children to "rank" a list of sins from the least to the worst. How do we commonly "measure" sin? On the cross, how did God measure different sins?

Who does your child have a hard time forgiving? Remind your child that forgiveness does not make light of an offense; it is a choice to no longer give the offense power in his or her life.

PRAYER NOTES AND PERSONAL REFLECTIONS

_____

_____

_____

_____

_____

_____

_____

_____

_____

_____

_____

_____

_____

_____

_____

_____

_____

_____

BROKEN RELATIONSHIPS

Reconciliation, Not Necessarily Restoration

As she got out of the car, Emily smiled at the two large, exuberant dogs bounding toward her. Dogs barking, dirt flying, daughter wailing—a sudden disaster unfolded before my eyes as Emily's knee split open on the gravel driveway. Three hours and six stitches later, Emily limped from the emergency room to the car. The next time we visited our friends, she was extremely guarded around their dogs! Six years later, a two-inch scar on her knee is a reminder of a lesson about boundaries and trust learned the hard way.

This incident simplistically illustrates a relational truth: When boundaries are overstepped, intentionally or unintentionally, people get hurt. Emily's wound healed fairly quickly but left a permanent mark on her. However, the wounds that lead to broken relationships are deeper and take longer to heal. They often leave invisible scars, reminding us that navigating the territory of boundaries and trust in relationships can be confusing and complicated. Mending broken relationships is a process; and sometimes when relationships are put back together, they are different than before.

Healing of relationships involves forgiveness, reconciliation and restoration—all biblical practices mirroring God's love relationship with us. But there is much confusion about these terms among Christian women, who often expend a great deal of emotional energy being "relationship fixers." When well-meaning people blindly bundle forgiveness, reconciliation and restoration together, using the terms interchangeably, they dishonor the nuances of relationship and disregard important distinctions between love, respect and trust.

Forgiveness, reconciliation and restoration are stand-alone pieces of the healing process. Forgiveness lets go of ill will toward another for a wrong suffered; reconciliation negotiates an acceptable way to reestablish the relationship; restoration repairs and rebuilds the relationship as it was originally intended to be. When we practice forgiveness and initiate reconciliation, we live out the love and grace God has shown us. Restoration, however, hinges on the lived-out repentance of the other and requires that healthy relational boundaries are clearly established, understood and observed.

Forgiveness requires love; reconciliation requires respect; restoration requires trust. The core essentials of mutual trust, love and respect are the secure three-legged foundation necessary for a relationship to thrive. If one or more of these is compromised, the process of restoration flounders. Restoration can only happen as the offender takes responsibility for wounding the other (confession) and lives out genuine change (repentance). The relationship is restored as consistent action over time demonstrates love, respect for healthy relational boundaries and trustworthiness.

Ever since Eden, sin has created broken relationships, with God and with others. The Bible is the love story of God's desire for us to be reconciled to Him and to one another. The Bible teaches that all healthy relationships have terms, or boundaries, that protect love and foster respect. Throughout the Old Testament, God's love for His people was unconditional, but His relationship with them was not without terms—*His* terms. The altar was a "table of reconciliation," a meeting place with God where sacrifices made atonement for sin, making fellowship between God and man possible.

The altar of the cross was the final "table of reconciliation"; Jesus was both the mediator and the sacrifice, negotiating once and for all a way for us to have fellowship with God. Through Christ's sacrificial death, forgiveness was offered, reconciliation initiated and the door of restoration opened. God provided the way for reconciliation, but restoration only happens when we admit our sin, accept His sacrifice for us and agree to live under His Lordship. Only then can we enjoy the relationship with Him that He intended from the beginning.

Seeking reconciliation with others reflects God's mercy and grace; offering forgiveness and setting boundaries in relationships honors His design for relationships characterized by love and respect. However, refusing to resume business-as-usual when trust has been compromised honors God's design for integrity in relationships. Unless broken trust is rebuilt through humility and responsibility, reconciliation will not necessarily mean restoration.

A Place of Reconciliation

*So if you are presenting a sacrifice at the altar in the Temple and
you suddenly remember that someone has something against you,
leave your sacrifice there at the altar. Go and be reconciled to that person.
Then come and offer your sacrifice to God.*
MATTHEW 5:23-24, *NLT*

*Therefore, if anyone is in Christ, he is a new creation; the old has gone,
the new has come! All this is from God, who reconciled us to himself
through Christ and gave us the ministry of reconciliation: that God was
reconciling the world to himself in Christ, not counting men's sins against them.
And he has committed to us the message of reconciliation.*
2 CORINTHIANS 5:17-19

*You were his enemies, separated from him by your evil thoughts and actions.
Yet now he has reconciled you to himself through the death of Christ in his
physical body. As a result, he has brought you into his own presence, and you
are holy and blameless as you stand before him without a single fault.*
COLOSSIANS 1:21-22, *NLT*

*For there is only one God and one Mediator who can reconcile
God and humanity—the man Christ Jesus.*
1 TIMOTHY 2:5, *NLT*

For Reflection

When we extend forgiveness we cannot presume reconciliation, and efforts toward reconciliation do not necessarily result in restoration.

Living at a Place Near His Altar

Consider the three-legged stool of love, respect and trust in relationships.
Examine which "leg" of the stool was hurt in a broken relationship.
Do you need to seek reconciliation in a relationship?

What boundaries do you need to create to maintain respect in that relationship?

What attitudes and behavioral changes do you need to see for trust to be restored?

INVITING YOUR CHILDREN TO HIS ALTAR

Your children will learn first from your example, then from your words. What is your example in teaching your children about reconciliation in relationships?

Family relationships are the laboratory where reconciliation skills are learned. Instead of brushing conflicts under the table or moving on without resolution, invite your children to the "negotiating table" to sort out their differences: *What happened, and how were feelings hurt? What boundaries were violated? What boundaries need to be honored? Does someone need to own an offense and offer an apology? What could have been done differently to demonstrate love and respect?*

If your children are not comfortable trusting someone, do not press them to do so. As you support their intuition, they learn to trust their God-given instincts, which may prove invaluable in the future.

PRAYER NOTES AND PERSONAL REFLECTIONS

_____
_____
_____
_____
_____
_____
_____
_____
_____
_____
_____

STARTING OVER

Returning to God After You've Walked Away

As I came around the corner of the church hallway, my friend Erin caught my eye.

Her eyes were red and brimming with tears; I could tell by the way she hugged me that she was hurting deeply.

"What's going on?" I asked, realizing it had been several months since we had met for lunch.

"I've really messed up," Erin blurted. Over the next few minutes she spilled her guilt over a recent affair with a married man. "I'm so ashamed. One thing just led to another . . ." Her voice trailed off, full of regret. She had not been to church for many months, but she knew it was now time to find her way back to God. Over the following weeks, we unraveled the tangled threads of choices that had led her down a very slippery slope.

We all mess up. Sometimes it's the result of barely noticeable, incremental, self-serving steps we've taken to assuage emotional pain or feed emotional needs. We wake up one day wondering, *How did I end up so far down this road?* Sometimes our mess is the result of deliberate, conscious choices we've made to chart our own course and serve our own personal agenda. Under a cascade of consequences, we realize we've royally botched up our lives. When we survey the damages, we wonder if this time we've messed up so much that there's no way to get things right again.

Jesus' parable of the prodigal son illustrates our predicament (see Luke 15). A young man with an attitude of entitlement, and driven by selfishness and pride, decided to leave home and do life his own way. Making up his own rules as he went along, he chased the life he thought he wanted. Only when he came to the end of his money, the end of his self-scripted solutions and the end of him*self* did he come to his senses: in chasing "the good life," he had forfeited the *truly* good life. Humbled and broken, he headed home empty-handed, with nothing to offer except an admission of his own foolishness and a plea to be taken on as a hired hand.

If we're honest, we've all walked in the young man's shoes at different points in life. Spurred on by selfishness and pride, we've tried our own life-solutions and have messed up in small ways and big ways; the result is a price tag of incalculable cost and insurmountable loss. We are left holding the pieces of a broken relationship with God, broken relationships with others and a broken view of ourselves. At the end of our brokenness, when we realize we cannot fix ourselves and we are bankrupt in every way, we want to head home—but can we? Entitled to nothing and with nothing to offer, we wonder if God will have anything to do with us.

As the young prodigal headed home, his father saw him in the distance, broke into a run and started throwing things—he threw his arms around him in love; he threw his cloak on him, covering his shame; and he threw a party for him, celebrating his return. The father loved the prodigal extravagantly and unconditionally and had waited for this day of reconciliation!

"Reconciliation" is a term used in accounting when balancing the books. On the altar of the cross, Jesus paid the debt that you and I could never pay. We have no credit of our own; God transferred our debt in full to His own Son. Our right relationship with God is all on the account of Jesus' blood, shed for our sin.

God saw my friend Erin's bankrupt condition all along and had been waiting for her to see it too. His eyes of compassion had been scanning the horizon, waiting for her to return home. No matter how many wrong turns you have taken, you only need to turn around to see the Father's outstretched arms. When you "declare bankruptcy" and humbly turn to the Father, He's already running toward you, throwing things. Let the celebration begin!

A PLACE OF RECONCILIATION

But while he was still a long way off, his father saw him and was filled with compassion for him; he ran to his son, threw his arms around him and kissed him. The son said to him, "Father, I have sinned against heaven and against you.

I am no longer worthy to be called your son." But the father said to his servants, "Quick! Bring the best robe and put it on him. Put a ring on his finger and sandals on his feet. Bring the fattened calf and kill it. Let's have a feast and celebrate. For this son of mine was dead and is alive again; he was lost and is found." So they began to celebrate.
LUKE 15:20-24

For God was in Christ, reconciling the world to himself, no longer counting people's sins against them. And he gave us this wonderful message of reconciliation. So we are Christ's ambassadors; God is making his appeal through us. We speak for Christ when we plead, "Come back to God!" For God made Christ, who never sinned, to be the offering for our sin, so that we could be made right with God through Christ.
2 CORINTHIANS 5:19-21, *NLT*

If we confess our sins, he is faithful and just and will forgive us our sins and purify us from all unrighteousness.
1 JOHN 1:9

FOR REFLECTION

Shame, the flip side of pride, sometimes hinders us from returning to God; humility brings us to Him empty-handed. His mercy embraces us on the path, His grace wraps us in His robes of righteousness and His unconditional love celebrates our homecoming.

LIVING AT A PLACE NEAR HIS ALTAR

When you have been tempted to do life your own way, what has been the result?

What incremental or intentional choices have you made that have created distance between you and God?

What keeps you from returning home to your heavenly Father?

INVITING YOUR CHILDREN TO HIS ALTAR

If you have prodigal children, don't give up "scanning the horizon" for their return in prayer. Pray that you will demonstrate God's grace and mercy to them.

What do your children need from you when they admit they have messed up? Do you offer them a lecture or a loving embrace? Do you throw guilt upon them or a cloak of forgiveness? Are you condescending toward them, or do you lift them up with encouragement?

Instead of saying, "I told you so!" say, "I love you so!"

PRAYER NOTES AND PERSONAL REFLECTIONS

_____

_____

_____

_____

_____

_____

_____

_____

_____

_____

_____

_____

_____

_____

_____

_____

_____

_____

_____

_____

CONTENTMENT

Acceptance in the Present and Hope for the Future

"Any chance of reconciliation?"

This was a question I was often asked during my marital separation. The notion that everything can ultimately be sorted out and put back together is one of the fragile strands of hope we hold on to in life. But sometimes we are left holding frayed, broken shoelaces instead. What does reconciliation look like when one party walks away, the relationship is permanently broken, and issues remain indefinitely unresolved?

Dictionaries offer many shades of meaning for the word "reconciliation": creating harmony; settling or resolving disputes; finding contentment. When relationships are left dangling, without resolution, "finding contentment" is the one-sided experience of reconciliation; it only requires acceptance. *Acceptance means reconciling oneself to the reality of what is and who the other is.* It means no longer rewriting the past, manipulating the present or trying to change the future of the relationship. Acceptance is a place of present contentment that I can choose; it is not dependent on another's choices or changes.

Wounds that tie us to the past, or a stubborn belief that our present and future wellbeing hinges on another, hinder us from finding contentment. Like oxen sharing a yoke, we chafe at the neck while struggling against the emotional pull and power of the "other," sometimes long after a relationship has been terminated. The obvious solution is to remove the yoke.

What keeps you emotionally connected to this person? Why do you continue to give this person emotional power in your life? Removing the yoke means letting go of the past through forgiveness, finding your identity in the present as a beloved child of God and entrusting your present and future wellbeing to His sovereign care. These choices enable you to experience emotional closure concerning the past, release you from the emotional control of another in the present, and empower you to move forward in emotional freedom.

Joseph knew the frustration of unresolved wounds and unrestored relationships (see Genesis 37–45,50). Sold into slavery by his abusive older brothers, Joseph had no recourse to address their cruelty. In Egypt, he was unjustly accused of immorality by Potiphar's wife and falsely imprisoned, with no opportunity to defend himself. Forgotten and forsaken in his solitary cell, he could have become emotionally imprisoned by bitterness, resentment and cynicism. However, years later, when Joseph was released from prison, he emerged as a man of humility, grace and faith in God's sovereign care—evidence that Joseph had experienced the solitary soul work of reconciliation, producing acceptance and contentment.

Joseph was eventually moved from prison to a position of power that would have enabled him to retaliate against his offenders. However, God had already repositioned Joseph's heart: entitlement was replaced by meekness. Though he had an opportunity to avenge his brothers' offense, Joseph chose forgiveness and confidence in God's sovereign care: "But don't be upset, and don't be angry with yourselves for selling me to this place. It was God who sent me here ahead of you to preserve your lives" (Genesis 45:5, *NLT*). Joseph later reassured them again saying, " 'Don't be afraid of me. Am I God, that I can punish you? You intended to harm me, but God intended it all for good. He brought me to this position so I could save the lives of many people. No, don't be afraid. I will continue to take care of you and your children.' So he reassured them by speaking kindly to them" (Genesis 50:19-21, *NLT*).

Joseph's attitudes and choices reveal a man who discovered the one-way path of reconciliation in the wake of unresolved relationships. The grace of God invites us to do the same. On the altar of the cross, Jesus Christ chose meekness over power, humility over pride and grace over retaliation toward those who crucified him, saying, "Father, forgive them, for they don't know what they are doing" (Luke 23:34, *NLT*).

He is the One who enables us to accomplish the solitary soul work of reconciliation, empowering us to live in the emotional freedom of acceptance and contentment.

A PLACE OF RECONCILIATION

An offended friend is harder to win back than a fortified city.
Arguments separate friends like a gate locked with bars.
PROVERBS 18:19, *NLT*

You're familiar with the old written law, "Love your friend," and its
unwritten companion, "Hate your enemy." I'm challenging that.
I'm telling you to love your enemies. Let them bring out the best in you,
not the worst. When someone gives you a hard time, respond with
the energies of prayer, for then you are working out of your
true selves, your God-created selves.
MATTHEW 5:43-44, *THE MESSAGE*

Dear friends, never take revenge. Leave that to the righteous anger of God.
For the Scriptures say, "I will take revenge; I will pay them back," says the LORD.
Instead, "If your enemies are hungry, feed them. If they are thirsty, give them
something to drink. In doing this, you will heap burning coals of shame on their
heads." Don't let evil conquer you, but conquer evil by doing good.
ROMANS 12:19-21, *NLT*

Watch out that no poisonous root of bitterness grows up
to trouble you, corrupting many.
HEBREWS 12:15, *NLT*

FOR REFLECTION

The path to acceptance and contentment is paved with trust in God's sovereign care. By God's grace, we can choose to become better rather than bitter.

LIVING AT A PLACE NEAR HIS ALTAR

How do you carry the past, challenge the present or try to change the future regarding an unresolved relationship in your life?

What keeps you from exchanging the yoke of emotional power and control for the yoke of acceptance and contentment?

What do you learn about reconciliation from the story of Joseph and the example of Jesus Christ?

INVITING YOUR CHILDREN TO HIS ALTAR

Ask your children to create a list of grievances that Joseph might have written while imprisoned. How would they respond to similar injustices? How might Jesus respond to those grievances?

When you have conflict with your children, forgive them long before they seek your forgiveness. By your example, they will learn that forgiveness does not hinge on another's repentance.

When your children struggle with an unresolved relationship, help them come to a place of acceptance by identifying what wounds need to be forgiven, determining what they can and cannot change and anchoring their identity in God's unconditional love.

PRAYER NOTES AND PERSONAL REFLECTIONS

_____

_____

_____

_____

_____

_____

_____

_____

_____

A PAINFUL PAST

Cleaning Out the Cluttered Corners of the Soul

For more than 40 years, I have been a dog person. I have always had a dog, since I was six years old. This week, I did the unthinkable. Because my daughter Emily passionately loves cats, we rescued a cat from a local animal shelter. We adopted her just three hours before she would have been euthanized. Appropriately, she is named "Grace."

Making room for the required cat paraphernalia of a litter box and a bed meant facing the formidable task of decluttering and cleaning out an unsightly corner of our laundry room. My foray into this catch-all corner unearthed leftovers from the past: unhung wall hangings, an old curtain rod (missing one bracket), a disassembled table, boxes of discarded toys intended for Goodwill and other miscellaneous items I have kept for no particular reason. I had become accustomed to the clutter and was generally able to look past it, though at times the mess was inconvenient or annoying. It was easier to ignore it than to interrupt life and deal with it; over time, the size of the task became daunting. But what had accumulated over a period of seven years, I actually cleaned out in a mere 15 minutes, *simply because I finally made a decision to get rid of it*—to make room for Grace. My laundry room is suddenly larger, more attractive and more functional. The cluttered corner has been redeemed for a new purpose. Why did I hang on to that stuff for so long?

Our external world sometimes reflects our internal world. What else have I been holding on to, only because I have not chosen to let go of it yet? Broken dreams, false hopes, picture-perfect illusions, unmet expectations, anger or resentment—vestiges of a past that cannot be changed can clutter the corners of my life, consume precious emotional energy, limit functionality and hinder God's grace from entering the nooks and crannies of my soul. *What do I gain by holding on to them?*

In addition, daily soul-clutter arrives uninvited like junk mail piling up on the emotional countertop of my life. Ungrounded fear, fruitless worry, unhealthy relationships, unrealistic expectations of myself or others—these shackle my spirit and weigh me down, depleting my energy and impeding my daily progress. Soul-clutter distracts me from God's good purposes, discourages my faith and defeats my ability to live in emotional freedom. It crowds out the only life that is truly life-giving—the life of the Spirit. Do I give these things a place in my life because I fear letting go of them? Do I accommodate them because I doubt God's goodness to me?

Jesus encountered a man who had been ill for 38 years (see John 5:5). Jesus had just one question for him: "Do you want to get well?" (v. 6). Ironically, the man responded with his "if only" list, a list that enabled him to remain an invalid. If only he could get into the healing waters of the Pool of Bethesda; if only he had someone to help him; if only others didn't have advantages over him. Jesus invited this man to make a decision, empowering him to choose wellbeing. Jesus poses the same question to those of us who hold on to a painful past and offers to empower us to let go and choose wellbeing.

Surrendering my soul-clutter at the foot of the cross means putting my past, present and future in God's good hands and trusting that He redemptively uses everything and doesn't waste anything. Whatever I am holding on to, in fact, has a hold on me. To receive the good that God offers me, I must first let go. Letting go means facing any unhealthiness I harbor, deciding it is a hindrance rather than help and choosing to grasp the reality of God's grace instead. Instead of looking back, I am free to press forward unencumbered on the course that Jesus sets before me.

The arrival in our home of amazing Grace has been accompanied by joy and laughter. Making a place for Grace reminds me that when I clean out the untended corners of my soul or clear off my emotional countertop, I expose places for God's redemptive grace to penetrate the corners of my life, reclaiming territory and reenergizing me for His good purposes. Receiving and embracing His grace, I make room for new beginnings that are accompanied by joy and laughter. Grace is good, all the time.

A PLACE OF REDEMPTION

I run in the path of your commands, for you have set my heart free.
PSALM 119:32

Let your eyes look straight ahead, fix your gaze directly before you.
Make level paths for your feet and take only ways that are firm.
PROVERBS 4:25-26

Search me, O God, and know my heart; test me and know my
anxious thoughts. Point out anything in me that offends you,
and lead me along the path of everlasting life.
PSALM 139:23-24, *NLT*

When Jesus saw him lying there and learned that he had been in this
condition for a long time, he asked him, "Do you want to get well?"
JOHN 5:6

Therefore, since we are surrounded by such a huge crowd of
witnesses to the life of faith, let us strip off every weight that slows us down,
especially the sin that so easily trips us up. And let us run
with endurance the race God has set before us.
HEBREWS 12:1, *NLT*

FOR REFLECTION

Jesus, the author of new beginnings, says to each of us, "Do you want to get well?"

LIVING AT A PLACE NEAR HIS ALTAR

What soul-clutter from the past do you harbor in the corners of your life?

What daily soul-clutter accumulates on the emotional countertop of your life?

How would your life be different if you surrendered these areas to God?

INVITING YOUR CHILDREN TO HIS ALTAR

Work together to clean out a closet or pantry. How will you decide what to keep, give away or throw away? Notice the difference when the project is complete! Talk about some soul-clutter you have decided to let go of and the difference that makes in your life.

What negative attitudes do your children hold on to? What keeps them from letting go of those attitudes?

Use trash recycling as an opportunity to talk with your children about some of the ways God can recycle our painful experiences to transform our lives. Share an example from your own life

PRAYER NOTES AND PERSONAL REFLECTIONS

GOD USES EVERYTHING

Nothing Is Wasted in God's Hands

Anita is an extraordinary sculptor; she is also a scavenger. Like Pixar's Wall-E, she sees potential and possibilities in the most unlikely discards. Her studio is a fascinating repository of found objects—old bicycles, abandoned baby dolls, a broken cello and a mishmash of other curbside cast-offs. Anita's creative, clever artistry redeems these found objects, turning "trash" into "treasure." *Does God see similar potential in my own life?*

Life during the two years of my separation and divorce process was like being shipwrecked during an extended hurricane season. As one storm wreaked havoc in our lives, another was brewing. My losses and those of my children hit like persistent waves. Struggling to stay afloat emotionally, I lived in survival mode, resisting the powerful undertow of each event. In my most difficult moments, a wise friend's words echoed in my ears: "God uses everything, and doesn't waste anything." *Really?* As I observed the flotsam and jetsam of our lives, holding on to that truism required a giant stretch of faith—believing that beyond the horizon of my circumstances, God could do the unimaginable, and hoping that beyond the scope of my vision, He would. Those moments required pressing into God's love, taking Him at His Word and leaning on His power and His promises day by day.

In time, the steady storms subsided, and we found our footing. But despite many wonderful blessings over the past eight years, the losses for me and my children have continued to roll in like waves hitting the beach. I have been reluctantly learning that the best way to ride waves of loss is to anticipate them, accept them and even embrace them.

Although it is counterintuitive to lean into loss, that is how I have discovered the embrace of God. In turbulent times, remember that He is the God of the waves, even the ones that ravage your world. The One who suffered loss for our sakes, rescues us, holds on to us, helps us and carries us; sometimes His rescue efforts are made more difficult by our flailing and struggling against Him. In the aftermath of the storm, as the waves recede, combing our losses means walking with God through the debris left behind—picking through the ruin to find what is valuable and salvageable as well as identifying what is not. It also means grieving what has been completely washed away and will never be the same.

As we bring our losses to the foot of the cross, we position ourselves to see God redeem them in unimagined ways. When Christ died on the cross, He paid the ultimate price to redeem us from the power of our slave master, sin, and began the ongoing work of redeeming us from the effects of sin in our lives. Our Creator-Redeemer pulls light out of darkness and new life out of death. God reminds us that His ways are not our ways, and His thoughts are higher than our thoughts (see Isaiah 55:8-9). Often His purposes are difficult to discern and more difficult to understand. His grand scheme always exceeds our greatest imagining.

Like a creative sculptor, God is using "found objects" that have washed ashore—gifts deposited by the waves—to shape His purposes in and through my life. Waves of fear left new faith and courage to step out in new directions and pursue a graduate degree in counseling. Waves of sorrow and pain deposited compassion and empathy, enabling me to offer understanding, grace and hope to an extraordinary sisterhood of women. Waves of confusion and disillusionment deposited clarity and fresh purpose as I worked with a team of people to establish Parenting Alone, a nonprofit community agency serving single-parent families. My life did not unfold the way I had dreamed as a young bride, but God is redemptively weaving the threads of my worst nightmare into life-giving dreams and hope-filled realities. His clever artistry uses everything I put in His hands, and doesn't waste anything. I marvel and wonder, and give thanks.

A PLACE OF REDEMPTION

They remembered that God was their Rock, that God
Most High was their Redeemer.
PSALM 78:35

When they walk through the Valley of Weeping, it will become a place of
refreshing springs. The autumn rains will clothe it with blessings.
PSALM 84:6, NLT

Don't be afraid, I've redeemed you. I've called your name. You're mine.
When you're in over your head, I'll be there with you. When you're in rough
waters, you will not go down. When you're between a rock and a hard place,
it won't be a dead end—Because I am God, your personal God, the Holy of
Israel, your Savior. I paid a huge price for you . . . That's how much
you mean to me! That's how much I love you!
ISAIAH 43:1-3, THE MESSAGE

In all their suffering he also suffered, and he personally rescued them.
In his love and mercy he redeemed them. He lifted them up and
carried them through all the years.
ISAIAH 63:9, NLT

Now all glory to God, who is able, through his mighty power at work within us,
to accomplish infinitely more than we might ask or think.
EPHESIANS 3:20, NLT

FOR REFLECTION

Creation is God's opening act in Genesis and His closing scene in Revelation. As we live in the chapters of time in-between, His ongoing, loving, redemptive work continues to salvage our lives, creating new beginnings out of tragic endings, wholeness out of brokenness and glorious purpose out of grief and pain.

LIVING AT A PLACE NEAR HIS ALTAR

As you comb your losses, what remains salvageable, and what is not?

What "found objects" will you put in God's hands to redeem?

How do you see God at work redeeming your losses?

INVITING YOUR CHILDREN TO HIS ALTAR

Using scraps of words and pictures cut from magazines and craft glue, create a collage on two-inch clay flowerpots; spray with an acrylic finish. Use as a planter or a votive candleholder. How can God creatively use the "scraps" of your life for good?

What household items can your family redeem for new purposes? See who can list the most ideas, and implement the most useful ones.

Visit a local recycling center or a salvage yard. Talk with your children about the ways that God "recycles" broken pieces of our lives for new purposes.

PRAYER NOTES AND PERSONAL REFLECTIONS

_____

_____

_____

_____

_____

_____

_____

_____

_____

_____

_____

DAY 33

LOSS

God Meets Us in the Broken Places

Humpty Dumpty sat on a wall, Humpty Dumpty had a great fall;
All the king's horses and all the king's men
Couldn't put Humpty Dumpty together again.

In childhood fairy tales, hope prevails. Eventually, "they all lived happily ever after." But real-life tales more closely resemble tragedy. Life breaks, and someone is left holding the broken pieces. What then?

As my car crept through the school zone, I offered my customary pray-out-loud-with-your-eyes-open-while-you-drive benediction to our morning scramble, asking God for good attitudes, success in tests and wisdom for my children's teachers. I tacked on an odd closing sentence: "I pray the events of today will cause us to trust You more. Amen." *Where did that thought come from?* I quickly glanced at the car clock; it was 7:47; the kids would have to hustle to be seated in their classrooms by 8:00 A.M.!

Shortly after I returned home, my sister called. "Turn on your TV! A plane has crashed into the World Trade Center!" Gripped by horror, fear and confusion, I watched the towers topple to their foundations. I thought of families whose worlds were crashing, forever changed, with untold ramifications. Fresh on the heels of my recent divorce, I sobbed for so many people who were suddenly single parents, and children without parents. The first plane hit the North Tower at 8:46 A.M. (EST), just moments before my peculiar prayer. *I pray the events of today will cause us to trust You more. Amen.*

When my own world crashed, I sat curled in a fetal position, thinking, "I will never be okay again." Previous losses had not prepared me for this utter devastation. *Or had they?* In fact, my earlier journeys through infertility, miscarriages, depression and marital struggles had taught me that when everything else crumbled, God's goodness, faithfulness and unfailing love remained impenetrable. Now, that foundation mattered more than ever! Our circumstances were forever altered, but God remained unchanged. Initially, I felt timid relying on God. After all, He had let this happen! But the prospect of walking into an unknown future without His help and guidance was utterly terrifying. *I pray the events of today will cause us to trust You more.*

"Martha said to Jesus, 'Lord, if only you had been here, my brother would not have died. But even now I know that God will give you whatever you ask'" (John 11:21, *NLT*). *Lord, You could have kept this from happening. But even the end isn't the end with You; even now You are able to do something.* Jesus wept—and moments later raised Lazarus from the dead, to the glory of God. Jesus weeps with us in our losses, intercedes for us and brings new life out of the deaths we surrender to Him—to the glory of God.

God draws near to the brokenhearted—so near that He entered our broken world and took our brokenness upon Himself on the cross. When life breaks, and we are left holding the pieces, we only have two options: we can attempt to put Humpty Dumpty together again by ourselves, or we can entrust the broken pieces of our lives to our Redeemer, at the foot of the cross. When we do, He gently gathers the pieces in His nail-pierced hands and promises to redeem them in ways we never dreamed possible. Our God of resurrection power is faithful to bring triumph out of tragedy.

"Whatever happened to living happily ever after?" I asked my dad, through tears, when my world crashed. Dad gently responded, "In the big picture of things, the 'happily ever after' that matters most of all is in Romans 8:29, 'to become like his Son.'"

That is the ultimate goal and triumph of God's redemptive work in our lives.

A PLACE OF REDEMPTION

The Lord is close to the brokenhearted; he rescues those
whose spirits are crushed.
PSALM 34:18, *NLT*

*That's why we can be so sure that every detail in our lives of love
for God is worked into something good. God knew what he was doing from the
very beginning. He decided from the outset to shape the lives of those who love
him along the same lines as the life of his Son. The Son stands
first in the line of humanity he restored. We see the original and intended
shape of our lives there in him. After God made that decision of what
his children should be like, he followed it up by calling people by name.
After he called them by name, he set them on a solid basis with himself.
And then, after getting them established, he stayed with them to the end,
gloriously completing what he had begun.*
ROMANS 8:28-30, *THE MESSAGE*

*Can anything ever separate us from Christ's love? Does it mean he no longer
loves us if we have trouble or calamity, or are persecuted, or hungry,
or destitute, or in danger, or threatened with death? . . . No, despite all these
things, overwhelming victory is ours through Christ, who loved us.*
ROMANS 8:35,37, *NLT*

FOR REFLECTION

Some say there are no tears in heaven; yet as surely as Jesus wept at
the grave of Lazarus, God grieves over the painful outcomes in our
lives. Our Creator-Redeemer, whose power is unlimited, creates new
beginnings for us, for the glory of God.

LIVING AT A PLACE NEAR HIS ALTAR

When did your world crash? In the aftermath, what foundation remained?

How can your personal crises prompt you to trust God more?

In the parable of the wise man who built his house upon the rock (see
Matthew 7:23-25), the house withstood the storm because of its foundation. What is your foundation today?

INVITING YOUR CHILDREN TO HIS ALTAR

Play the game Jenga with your children. When is the tower most likely to topple, and what keeps it stable? When your plans topple, what keeps your lives stable?

Invite your children to help you with a recipe that uses eggs. Point out that when the eggshell breaks, it cannot be put back together, but something good remains. When the egg is added to other ingredients, something new and wonderful is produced. What good things have come out of the difficulties your children have experienced?

Provide journals for your children to write letters to God. Remind them that God knows, understands and is attentive to all their feelings, whether they are happy, sad, fearful, anxious, lonely, excited or hopeful.

PRAYER NOTES AND PERSONAL REFLECTIONS

SPIRITUAL HEALING

Safeguarding Your Soul

I collapsed into bed after my midnight run to pick up my daughter at the airport. It had been a 21-hour day, and I faded fast once my head hit the pillow.

"Mom! Mom! Come here!" Bethany Joy's urgent calls sounded far away—was I dreaming? Moments later, she bounded into my room carrying a large canvas bag normally stored on my closet shelf. "Mom, the stuff that was stolen—it's here, in this bag! The burglars left it in my room; I didn't see it at first because it was behind a large box." Suddenly I was wide awake, my heart racing as I stared down at the laptop computer and my jewelry box—unbelievable! Our home had been broken into the previous week; the police suggested the burglars were interrupted on the job by our arrival home. Apparently, they had left these items behind rather than get caught red-handed!

You just never know the unexpected ways that God will restore what has been lost! Although the items had never really left our house, they were definitely lost to us until my daughter recovered them. In actuality, they had been displaced and concealed by the burglars. The police had checked her room, but the items were obscured from view.

In the crisis of my separation and divorce, another Thief rummaged through my soul and left our lives in disarray. He created emotional upheaval and robbed us of security and trust, and our individual versions of "happily ever after." Presently, there are days when my world seems up-ended and my soul is invaded by an enemy that would rob me of joy, peace, hope, wisdom and love. His lies lead me down self-reliant, crooked paths that deny God's goodness, subvert His truth and deviate from His purposes. Jesus said, "The thief comes to steal, kill, and destroy" (John 10:10).

After the burglary, we made an inventory list of the missing items, and the police dusted for fingerprints. I focused on putting our home back in order and making it more secure. In the same way, there are ways to restore my soul to order, and preventative measures I can take to protect my soul from being vandalized. The Thief leaves his fingerprints everywhere, enabling me to notice my point of vulnerability. I must first acknowledge the disarray of my own soul; taking an inventory of the fruit of the Spirit that are "missing" reveals my point of need. Feelings of shame or guilt may point to ways that I have violated God's Word. At the foot of the cross, the Restorer of my soul takes my inventory list and offers me forgiveness and freedom; most of all, He offers me Himself. By His wounds, I am healed. But that is only the beginning.

Dusting for the fingerprints of the Thief exposes where he wriggles into my life. What doors to my soul do I leave unlocked for the Intruder by failing to rely on the Holy Spirit to guard my heart and mind with the security of God's promises? What careless thinking patterns that deny truth leave me wide open to his deceptive lies? What emotional needs tempt me to doubt God's sufficiency, unfailing love and faithfulness?

Detecting where the Thief has found my point of vulnerability enables me to humbly make adjustments in that area to restore my relationship with God and take preventative measures to thwart the Thief's subtle tactics in the future. Sometimes I need to make physical changes, such as getting more sleep to avoid fatigue. Sometimes I need to create emotional safety by establishing healthier relational boundaries to protect myself or reaching out to a friend to avoid the loneliness and isolation that sets me up to listen to the lies of the Thief. Sometimes I need to make some spiritual adjustments, such as meditating on a promise or committing to the disciplines of Bible reading, prayer or accountability to a trusted friend.

I have discovered that as my "house" is put in order at the foot of the cross, it isn't long before the "missing items" of joy, peace, wisdom, hope or love are restored. Many times, they were merely misplaced and hidden from view in all the upheaval.

A PLACE OF RESTORATION

*The Lord is my shepherd, I shall not be in want. He makes me lie down
in green pastures, he leads me beside quiet waters, he restores my soul.
He guides me in paths of righteousness for his name's sake.*
PSALM 23:1-3

*The LORD will guide you continually, giving you water when you are dry
and restoring your strength. You will be like a well-watered garden, like an
ever-flowing spring. Some of you will rebuild the deserted ruins of your cities.
Then you will be known as a rebuilder of walls and a restorer of homes.*
ISAIAH 58:11-12, *NLT*

*The thief comes only to steal and kill and destroy; I have come that
they may have life, and have it to the full.*
JOHN 10:10, *NIV*

*Therefore, put on every piece of God's armor so you will be able to resist the
enemy in the time of evil. Then after the battle you will still be standing firm.*
EPHESIANS 6:13, *NLT*

*So humble yourselves before God. Resist the devil, and he will flee from you.
Come close to God, and God will come close to you.*
JAMES 4:7-8, *NLT*

FOR REFLECTION

Our greatest challenge is to make time for introspection, self-reflection,
enemy detection and divine direction. The God who is for us is faithful to restore us!

LIVING AT A PLACE NEAR HIS ALTAR

What has the Thief "robbed" you of recently?

What is your personal point of vulnerability, and what adjustments
can you make to guard against the enemy's tactics?

Confess the ways you have yielded to the enemy instead of yielding to the Holy Spirit's power.

INVITING YOUR CHILDREN TO HIS ALTAR

Although our children need to be aware of Satan's manipulations, guard against attitudes that foster fear. Remind your children that "the Spirit who lives in you is greater than the spirit who lives in the world" (1 John 4:4, *NLT*).

Saying "The devil made me do it" is a cop-out. Challenge your children to take responsibility for their choices. What "lies" did they believe when they were making wrong choices?

Help your children learn that physical and emotional needs can undermine their attitudes and behaviors. When bad attitudes are evident, H-A-L-T. Ask: Am I Hungry? Angry? Lonely? Tired?

PRAYER NOTES AND PERSONAL REFLECTIONS

CHASING WIND

Finding Fullness in Christ

Three words permeated the news of Wall Street during the fall of 2008: "bankrupt," "buyout," and "bailout." As major financial institutions began imploding, a financial house of cards was collapsing. The frenzied productivity and perception of success of these institutions lacked the internal underpinnings to sustain them.

We have our own frenzied productivity that mimics what happened on Wall Street. Like the hammer of the bell that opens trading on the stock market, our alarm clock goes off in the morning, and the scramble begins. Our days are characterized by hedging bets in decision-making and managing futures (our kids'). Time and energy are the commodities we trade most often; we trade stocks called approval, significance and emotional or financial security—hoping that balancing these investments will yield short- and long-term returns. At the end of the day, we collapse into bed knowing that when the bell strikes in the morning, we will do it all over again.

On the outside, our lives look full; meanwhile, we debit and diminish our physical, emotional and spiritual resources. Responding to the demands of daily life, we give out more than we take in; we become depleted and eventually "bankrupt." We discover that however we measure success—money that stretches to the end of the month, a happy teenager or being super-mom of the week—it does not ultimately deliver a sense of true fullness to ourselves or our children, and in fact often does the opposite. All our frazzled busyness may be constructing a house of cards; our best efforts are invested in areas that provide variable returns that can be blown away with one bad day. On the outside, our lives look full; but on the inside, we are desperately empty.

Human nature hasn't changed much over time; the prophet Isaiah spoke to the same issues in his day: "Why spend money on what is not bread, and your labor on what does not satisfy?" (Isaiah 55:2). King Solomon called it "chasing after wind." The temporal cannot satisfy the spiritual; God works out of a different paradigm, using a different economy of energy and resources. Jesus said that if we seek our own life, we will lose it; instead, we have to lose our life—in Him—to find it. He promises that whatever we give up, leave behind or let go of to serve His purposes, He will return to us a hundredfold. He tells us to "be still" and "wait"—words that are contrary to our anxious nature—to be replenished and restored. These paradoxes of faith seem confusing, because we have been doing life backwards for so long. But when we find our life in our relationship with God, He offers us His unconditional love, security and significance at the front end. Then He fills us to overflowing with His Spirit to energize us for His purposes—purposes that pour eternal significance into the daily rhythms of our life and squeeze eternal value out of ordinary opportunities. His resources are never depleted, and the more we give out of His resources, the greater the dividends, both in this life and the life to come.

The amazing mystery of God's love is that Jesus, who embodied the fullness of God, "emptied Himself" (see Philippians 2:5-8) to give us fullness—an inner fullness that all the activity on earth can never produce. He saw our bankrupt condition and offered Himself as the buyout—His own life the purchase price to rescue us from our empty way of life. From the foot of the cross flows a river of living water that renews, restores and refreshes us. Each day, as we feed on His Word and ask His Holy Spirit to fill us, He deposits His eternal resources in our reserves and generates the power we need to live out His purposes. Apart from Him, we can only build a house of cards.

A PLACE OF RESTORATION

Unless the Lord builds a house, the work of the builders is wasted.
Unless the Lord protects a city, guarding it with sentries will do no good.
It is useless for you to work so hard from early morning until late at night,
anxiously working for food to eat; for God gives rest to his loved ones.
PSALM 127:1-2, *NLT*

My child, pay attention to what I say. Listen carefully to my words.
Don't lose sight of them. Let them penetrate deep into your heart, for they
bring life to those who find them, and healing to their whole body. Guard your
heart above all else, for it determines the course of your life.
PROVERBS 4:20-23, *NLT*

Come, all you who are thirsty, come to the waters; and you who have
no money, come, buy and eat! Come, buy wine and milk without money
and without cost. Why spend money on what is not bread, and your labor
on what does not satisfy? Listen, listen to me, and eat what is good,
and your soul will delight in the richest of fare.
ISAIAH 55:1-2

On the last day, the climax of the festival, Jesus stood and shouted to the crowds,
"Anyone who is thirsty may come to me! Anyone who believes in me may come and
drink! For the Scriptures declare, 'Rivers of living water will flow from his heart.'"
JOHN 7:37-38, *NLT*

For you know that God paid a ransom to save you from the empty life you
inherited from your ancestors. And the ransom he paid was not mere gold or
silver. It was the precious blood of Christ, the sinless, spotless Lamb of God.
1 PETER 1:18-19, *NLT*

FOR REFLECTION

Fullness isn't a by-product of our productivity; fullness is a prerequisite for living productively, through God's power.

LIVING AT A PLACE NEAR HIS ALTAR

How do you measure "success"?

To what substitute paths do you turn to find "fullness" (relationships, food, work, exercise, your children)?

How have you been living life "backward"?

INVITING YOUR CHILDREN TO HIS ALTAR

Ask your children to describe a full and satisfying day. Does their answer reflect a balance of time invested in activities, relationships and personal time?

Carefully weigh the investment of time in your child's extracurricular activities against the return value. Ask your children periodically what benefits they derive from their activities, and help them choose activities wisely.

Invite your children to enjoy "stillness" by watching a sunrise or a sunset, looking for shapes in the clouds or taking a nature walk.

PRAYER NOTES AND PERSONAL REFLECTIONS

_____

_____

_____

_____

_____

_____

_____

_____

_____

_____

_____

_____

_____

_____

_____

_____

_____

RUNNING ON EMPTY

Being Refueled Daily

I glanced at the fuel gauge and groaned, remembering that the warning light had come on the previous evening, on my way home. How many miles had I driven today without noticing this little warning light? I desperately prayed that I could make it to the nearest gas station.

"Running on fumes" seems to be the metaphor of my life as a single mom, and of life in America. A crazy schedule keeps me on the run, like the Energizer Bunny—except my battery runs out a lot sooner. I'm drained by the number of plates I'm spinning—by their weight and how fast they are spinning. Sometimes I get to control those factors by saying "no," "later," or asking others for help. Other times, I'm subject to people and powers beyond my control and just have to keep spinning the plates for a certain amount of time. Sometimes, a few of the plates drop, creating a mess. Occasionally, unexpected plates fly at me: a sick child, a funeral to attend or dealing with a broken-down car. Life happens, crises happen, but I somehow keep going. It is more than easy to run through life not noticing the light that warns me I am running on fumes.

Martha knew what it was like to give beyond her resources; she hit her tipping point while she was throwing an impromptu dinner party for Jesus and a dozen or so of his companions. Sometime during the course of her food preparations, her dinner party turned into a pity party. She felt overwhelmed, tired, resentful and irritated. Especially with Mary, her sister, but perhaps even a bit with Jesus.

I've been working my tail off getting everything ready while Mary is having a nice fireside chat with Jesus. Would it be too much for her to help out a bit? There's so much that needs to be done in so little time! Doesn't Jesus see how hard I'm trying to serve Him and everyone else? Doesn't He care?

Martha finally blurted out her frustrations to Jesus. "Martha, Martha," He replied, smoothing her ruffled feathers. "You are worried and upset about many things, but only one thing is needed. Mary has chosen what is better, and it will not be taken away from her" (Luke 10:41-42). *"Only ONE thing is needed"*—was He serious? Very. In our convoluted world where busyness masquerades as fullness, Jesus gently spoke to the heart of the problem—the problem of the heart. Our hearts can be so well-intended yet *un*tended!

Martha was industrious, hospitable and concerned for the needs of others—all wonderful qualities we esteem in others. But distracted by her concerns, she failed to address her own primary need. Mary, however, "got it." Mary understood that she had to tend her soul before she could tend to the demands of the day. Mary hung on Jesus' words because that's where she found Life. Unless she took Life in, she could not do life effectively.

Like my gas gauge, God does not demand my attention and is easily ignored in the busyness of life. Just as cars were not intended to run without fuel, God never intended for us to live apart from being empowered by His life. From the very beginning, God's plan was to restore our broken relationship with Him through Christ's death on the cross, and to fill us with His Spirit. As we worship at His feet daily, nourished by His Word and refreshed by His Holy Spirit, we are refueled with His wisdom, comfort, encouragement, promises and perspective—which we desperately need throughout each day.

A PLACE OF RESTORATION

*Satisfy us in the morning with your unfailing love, that we may
sing for joy and be glad all our days.*
PSALM 90:14

*Even youths will become weak and tired, and young men will fall in
exhaustion. But those who trust in the LORD will find new strength.
They will soar high on wings like eagles. They will run and not
grow weary. They will walk and not faint.*
ISAIAH 40:30-31, *NLT*

*Come to me with your ears wide open. Listen, and you will find life.
I will make an everlasting covenant with you. I will give you all the
unfailing love I promised to David.*
ISAIAH 55:3, *NLT*

*Remain in me, and I will remain in you. For a branch cannot produce
fruit if it is severed from the vine, and you cannot be fruitful unless you
remain in me. Yes, I am the vine; you are the branches. Those who
remain in me, and I in them, will produce much fruit. For apart from me
you can do nothing.... I have told you these things so that you
will be filled with my joy. Yes, your joy will overflow!*
JOHN 15:4-5,11, *NLT*

*May you experience the love of Christ, though it is too great to
understand fully. Then you will be made complete with all the fullness
of life and power that comes from God.*
EPHESIANS 3:19, *NLT*

FOR REFLECTION

"If I fail to spend two hours in prayer each morning, the devil gets the victory through the day. I have so much business I cannot get on without spending three hours daily in prayer" (Martin Luther).

LIVING AT A PLACE NEAR HIS ALTAR

What plates are you spinning? Do you need to say "no," "later" or "please help" to manage your time and energy more effectively?

What consequences do you experience when you are running on empty?

Routines help establish our priorities. What routine do you have in place for sitting at Jesus' feet to be restored by through His Word, worship, and prayer?

INVITING YOUR CHILDREN TO HIS ALTAR

Using your cell phone and charger as a visual aid, relate your children's need to be recharged. Discuss the negative consequences of "running on empty—fatigue, negative attitudes, interpersonal conflict.

Pay attention to your child's need for "down time." Pockets of unstructured time in your child's schedule enhance opportunities for creativity and enhance opportunities to exercise creativity and imagination.

Set an example for your children through your own daily Bible reading and prayer time. Ask them to honor that time by avoiding unnecessary interruptions. Provide your children with age-appropriate Bibles, youth devotional books and Christian literature to nourish them spiritually.

PRAYER NOTES AND PERSONAL REFLECTIONS

❦

REMOVING THE IDOLS

Identifying What Gets in the Way of God

With my first wave of consciousness, my thoughts galloped like wild stallions out of the starting gate, jumping the gun of my alarm clock. My to-do list was long; what remained unfinished from yesterday would have to be squeezed into today's already full schedule. Never mind that my eyes were still glued shut, my body still plastered to my mattress and a dull headache was slowly creeping across the crown of my head. *What does it mean to live today at the foot of the cross?* The unexpected question interrupted my racing thoughts; another question quickly followed: *What* distracts *me from living at the foot of the cross?* I mentally reviewed the previous day; anything and everything, it seems!

Single moms are the busiest, hardest-working people I know. They rise up early, stay up late and do an amazing juggling act in between, putting any circus clown to shame. Often, our lives do resemble a circus as we tame the lion (our boss) in one ring, teach dog tricks in another (our kids) and see how many stacking cups we can balance on our outstretched palms in ring number three (our home, family, friends, school and church commitments). Sometimes we fly on the trapeze for a little while with a "significant other," though many women don't even try adding that act—there's already enough clamoring for their attention, time and energy on the circus floor.

Distractions and competing interests abound. The whims of a child, the whining of a boss, well-intentioned commitments or the wooing of a significant other pull at us. As we arrange our life around good things in our three-ring circus, the good things can become our focal point, ends in themselves, consuming our energy, time and attention. They persuasively beckon us to do more, work harder, perform better and dance faster, while offering the validating kickbacks of approval, applause, affirmation and affection—if we just do "enough." Focused on these things, I find myself running in circles and veer off the true path of Life. *No wonder I am so tired; no wonder not everything on my to-do list gets done.*

God's Word reminds me that children, work, commitments and relationships are gifts from the Giver of Life, providing opportunities to love, serve and honor Him. But they are not meant to displace Him as my source of validation, purpose and fulfillment. When they do, they become idols. They are not ends in themselves, nor a means to finding "life," but a means of serving the One "in [whom] we live and move and have our being" (Acts 17:28). On the cross, the One who is Life gave His life for me that I might find my life in Him. He is the Source of my life, and His voice is the one I need to listen to above all others.

That early morning, I reined in my "galloping horses," mentally placing my to-do list at the foot of the cross. The One who wisely ordered the universe orders my life when I allow Him. In the quiet of my darkened room, I listened for what I almost missed—reminders from the Spirit that He loves me for who I am, not for what I do. It was like getting a good-morning hug; wrapped in His love, I loved Him back with words of worship. *It's not about me or my kids or my work or anything else. It's all about Him.* Humbling myself, I invited the "circus master" to be center stage in my day; I asked Him to sort my to-do list, adding and deleting to reflect His agenda. After my false start, I was ready to begin the day—attentive to Him and available for Him to do His work through me. Living today at the foot of the cross is my act of worship.

A PLACE OF WORSHIP

You have made known to me the path of life; you will fill me with joy in your presence, with eternal pleasures at your right hand.
PSALM 16:11

So here's what I want you to do, God helping you: Take your everyday, ordinary life—your sleeping, eating, going-to-work, and walking-around life—and place it before God as an offering. Embracing what

*God does for you is the best thing you can do for him. Don't become
so well-adjusted to your culture that you fit into it without even thinking.
Instead, fix your attention on God. You'll be changed from the inside out.
Readily recognize what he wants from you, and quickly respond to it.
Unlike the culture around you, always dragging you down to
its level of immaturity, God brings the best out of you, develops
well-formed maturity in you.*
ROMANS 12:1-2, *THE MESSAGE*

*So if you're serious about living this new resurrection life with Christ,
act like it. Pursue the things over which Christ presides. Don't shuffle along,
eyes to the ground, absorbed with the things right in front of you. Look up,
and be alert to what is going on around Christ—that's where the
action is. See things from his perspective.*
COLOSSIANS 3:1-2, *THE MESSAGE*

*Dear children, keep away from anything that might take
God's place in your hearts.*
1 JOHN 5:21, *NLT*

FOR REFLECTION

God loves me with a jealous love; worshiping the gift instead of the
Giver is idolatry.

LIVING AT A PLACE NEAR HIS ALTAR

What distractions muffle the voice of the Spirit in your life?

What good things can become "idols" to you, displacing God as your
source of life, validation and fulfillment? What kickbacks do those
good things offer you?

How can you give each item on today's to-do list to the Lord as an act
of worship?

INVITING YOUR CHILDREN TO HIS ALTAR

Talk with your children about sources of significance and worth: sports; cliques; social status; designer labels; grades; awards and merits. Weigh the kickbacks these offer, and their lasting value.

What people or pursuits displace God as the source of value and fulfillment in your children's lives?

Help your children identify their gifts and abilities. Discuss the ways they could use these gifts and abilities for selfish ends or to honor the Lord and serve others.

PRAYER NOTES AND PERSONAL REFLECTIONS

_____
_____
_____
_____
_____
_____
_____
_____
_____
_____
_____
_____
_____
_____
_____
_____
_____
_____
_____

OFFERING MYSELF

Leftovers, or a Living Sacrifice?

"What's for dinner, Mom?" Emily's inconvenient question interrupted my train of thought and brought me up short. *Was it that time already?* I foraged for any leftovers lurking in the fridge that I could hastily label "dinner." A twinge of guilt swept over me. *What message does my lack of planning, attentiveness and enthusiasm send to Emily about where she stands in my priorities?* Too often, dinner preparation is an obligatory ritual punctuating the end of the day. I zapped an odd assortment of leftovers in the microwave, knowing that my meager offering would be received with an equal lack of enthusiasm.

Unfortunately, I fall into this pattern with God, too. What leftovers do I give Him? Do I intentionally consider how I will serve Him, or do I throw together some last-minute obligatory token of service when He interrupts my busyness? Routines of daily Bible reading, prayer, and weekly church attendance can all become empty rituals offering a nod in His direction—or, they can be meaningful acts of worship. Likewise, running errands for my family, serving at church, helping a friend in a tight spot or going the extra mile at work can be enthusiastically motivated by love for God, or merely dutiful roles and responsibilities I fulfill as a "good Christian" mother, neighbor or coworker. The difference is purely in my motivation and attitude.

In the Old Testament, God required and received the first and best from His people, whether bringing an unblemished lamb or the first fruits of the harvest to the altar. The cream of the crop was consecrated, or set apart, for God, honoring His worth. These acts of worship were neither cavalier nor convenient; offerings were not haphazard or happenstance. Intentional and purposeful preparation and planning demonstrated that every area of life revolved around God.

Then and now, God has always looked past outward activity and appearances to the inclination of the heart. God was offended by sacrifices His people offered out of obligation, mimicking pagans who appeased and curried favor with their impersonal gods. God passionately loves us and desires worship that is motivated by love. Left to our own devices, our hearts run cold, our motives become self-serving and rituals become perfunctory performances. But our habits become holy habits when they are infused with the love of God and love for God. The command to love Him with all our heart, soul, and strength permeates our everyday, not-so-religious life (see Deuteronomy 6:5).

On the cross, Jesus, the unblemished Lamb of God, *willingly* offered Himself as the sacrifice for our sin—not out of obligation, but in humility and love. In response to His great mercy, Paul exhorts us to reciprocate by offering our bodies to God as "living sacrifices" (Romans 12:1). Jesus took on a human body to live out God's love for us in tangible ways. Likewise, as "living sacrifices" we are to live out His radical love for us—not just talk about it, think about it or feel it. Willing service offered as an expression of worship will change the way we view ourselves and others.

In the tedium of daily life, God does not delight in my obligatory offerings and daily leftovers. He desires a mutual loving-giving relationship with me. As He willingly laid Himself on the cross, I can choose to lay myself on His altar, motivated by my love and in response to His love. As this love bleeds into every nook and cranny of my daily attitudes and actions, all of life becomes an act of worship and a pleasing aroma to Him.

A PLACE OF WORSHIP

Going through the motions doesn't please you, a flawless performance
is nothing to you. I learned God-worship when my pride was shattered.
Heart-shattered lives ready for love don't for a moment escape God's notice.
Make Zion the place you delight in, repair Jerusalem's broken-down walls.
Then you'll get real worship from us, acts of worship small and large,
including all the bulls they can heave onto your altar!
PSALM 51:16-19, *THE MESSAGE*

*To love him with all your heart, with all your understanding
and with all your strength, and to love your neighbor as yourself is
more important than all burnt offerings and sacrifices.*
MARK 12:33

*And so, dear brothers and sisters, I plead with you to give your bodies to God
because of all he has done for you. Let them be a living and holy sacrifice—
the kind he will find acceptable. This is truly the way to worship him.*
ROMANS 12:1, *NLT*

*If I give everything I own to the poor and even go to the stake to be burned
as a martyr, but I don't love, I've gotten nowhere. So, no matter what I say, what
I believe, and what I do, I'm bankrupt without love.*
1 CORINTHIANS 13:3, *THE MESSAGE*

FOR REFLECTION

This paradox of simultaneously dying and living is the mystery of the
Christian life: only as I die to myself can I live to God.

LIVING AT A PLACE NEAR HIS ALTAR

What "leftovers" do you give to God? Ask God to reveal any spiritual
sluggishness that hinders your relationship with Him.

Are your daily "religious rituals" motivated by love (heart) or obligation (habit)? Ask God to purify your motives.

Our words often reveal whether our motivation is duty or desire.
Change your language to reflect the motivation of your heart. Instead
of saying, "I should help out," or "I should read my Bible more," say,
"I want to help out" and "I want to read my Bible more."

INVITING YOUR CHILDREN TO HIS ALTAR

Have a meal of leftovers; ask your children to identify some of the ways they give God and others "leftovers." Share an example from your own life.

Simple advance preparations can improve the attitudes you take to worship on Sunday. Start preparing on Saturday evening: avoid late bedtimes, select clothes, announce your departure time for church, and set out breakfast foods.

Play the "Should Game" for a week. When someone says, "I (you) should . . ." respond, "Yes, but do you (I) want to?" Keep a tally; the one with the least number of "shoulds" wins an activity of their choice—for example, a game night, making ice cream sundaes, or renting a favorite movie).

PRAYER NOTES AND PERSONAL REFLECTIONS

WORSHIP

Consecrating Daily Life

A hectic week culminated in a busy weekend and a chaotic Sunday morning. I settled into my seat at church anticipating a time of calm reflection. But instead, the stanzas of Frances Havergal's familiar hymn drew a disturbing contrast to my life.

"Take my life and let it be consecrated, Lord, to thee. . . " All week long, my life had been divided into little pieces and given away to the highest bidder. "Take my hands and let them move at the impulse of thy love . . ." Was God's love the driving force in all my busyness? "Take my feet and let them be swift and beautiful for thee . . ." I had dragged my feet in several areas of responsibility recently. "Take my lips and let them be filled with messages for thee . . . " Surely, my sharp scolding that morning had not blessed my daughter or my Lord. "Take my silver and my gold, not a mite would I withhold . . ." I winced, realizing I had forgotten a check for the morning offering plate. "Take myself and I will be ever, only, all for thee"; this was how Jesus both lived and died, with single-minded devotion. But as a living sacrifice, I am perpetually crawling off the altar. I prayed that the love of the Father and the power of the Holy Spirit would tether me to the altar of the cross, drawing me back from distractions to Himself.

The word "consecrated" means "set apart," conjuring up images of my great-grandmother's fine china and my grandmother's silver flatware, which I "set apart" to serve special guests on special occasions. But in Christ, every day is a special occasion for serving Him and others. Instead of giving my life away in little pieces to the highest bidder demanding my attention, I am called to give my life away to *Him,* to do *His* bidding.

The Bible describes single women from all walks of life who were consecrated to God. Dorcas had a reputation for "always doing good," making garments for widows (see Acts 9:36). Are my hands busy loving and serving others? The woman at the well ran to invite others to listen to Jesus (see John 4:28); am I willing to go out of my way to tell someone about Jesus? Miriam was a prophetess who spoke God's truth and celebrated God's activity with singing and dancing (see Exodus 15:20-21). Do I faithfully speak God's truth, and does praise spill off my lips when I see God at work? Luke wrote of a prostitute who washed Jesus' feet with expensive perfume and tears (see Luke 7:37-38) and a poor widow who gave her last nickel to God (see Luke 21:2-4). Jesus made examples of their extravagant worship, teaching others to love Him with abandon. What do I hold on to that God would have me let go of out of love for Him?

Jesus became the "highest bidder" on my life when He paid the price of His life on the cross for me—His life for my life. Out of pure gratitude for His love, my only reasonable response is to offer Him my life, embracing every opportunity as a daily act of worship (see Romans 12:1). The result is transformational, conforming me to His image and His purposes, producing joy and fullness of life and leaving a legacy for my children as they see my love for God fleshed out in word and deed.

"Take my life and let it be consecrated, Lord, to Thee."

A PLACE OF WORSHIP

But Samuel replied, "What is more pleasing to the Lord: your burnt offerings and sacrifices or your obedience to his voice? Listen! Obedience is better than sacrifice, and submission is better than offering the fat of rams."
1 SAMUEL 15:22, *NLT*

The sacrifice you desire is a broken spirit. You will not reject a broken and repentant heart, O God.
PSALM 51:17, *NLT*

In the same way, let your good deeds shine out for all to see, so that everyone will praise your heavenly Father.
MATTHEW 5:16, *NLT*

*My command is this: Love each other as I have loved you. Greater love
has no one than this, that he lay down his life for his friends.*
JOHN 15:12-13

So whether you eat or drink, or whatever you do, do it all for the glory of God.
1 CORINTHIANS 10:31, *NLT*

*Through Jesus, therefore, let us continually offer to God a sacrifice of praise—
the fruit of lips that confess his name.*
HEBREWS 13:15

*We know what real love is because Jesus gave up his life for us. So we also ought
to give up our lives for our brothers and sisters . . . Dear children, let's not
merely say that we love each other; let us show the truth by our actions.*
1 JOHN 3:16,18, *NLT*

FOR REFLECTION

Ordinary opportunities become acts of worship as I live out my love
for God through my words and actions.

LIVING AT A PLACE NEAR HIS ALTAR

Who or what were the "highest bidders" in your life this past week?

Reflect on the lyrics of the hymn "Take My Life and Let It Be" (available online if you do not own a hymnal). Ask God to show you specific ways you can apply each stanza to your life.

How can you use a current life situation as a special occasion to respond to God's love?

INVITING YOUR CHILDREN TO HIS ALTAR

Create a list with your children of things that are set apart in your
lives (for example, dishes used for special occasions, holiday traditions,

a savings account). Ask them to comment on what it means for their lives to be set apart for God.

Ask each of your children to draw their body outline on paper. Have them fill in the outline with examples of ways they can use their bodies for God (for example, coins in the hand to represent putting money in the offering plate; a smile and positive words to represent lips that encourage others; running shoes on their feet to represent quick obedience). Encourage your child to choose an area to work on each week.

Using shoelaces to tie a bow, explain that Jesus always tied love and obedience together. One without the other is flimsy and incomplete; try tying a bow with only one end of the shoelace! When your children disobey, gently remind them that obedience is one way they demonstrate their love for you, just as obeying God is a way we show our love for Him.

Prayer Notes and Personal Reflections

RELINQUISHING CONTROL

Freedom in Surrendering Outcomes

This week *everything* is breaking. My watch. My car. My refrigerator. My handy food processor (now discontinued). Worst of all, my communication with my daughter. I am tired, discouraged, frustrated and annoyed by the irritating reminder that life breaks—sometimes due to my own foolishness, and often in very dear, costly or inconvenient places. The breakage I see and experience outside of me pales in comparison with the internal emotional breakage, which I vainly mask. When life breaks, I can become plagued by guilt, worry, frustration, fear, grief or just the overwhelming feeling that *life is utterly unmanageable.*

Our management-oriented culture tells us otherwise, in everything from financial planning and weight loss to educating our children and cultivating spirituality. With our culture's emphasis on targeted outcomes, strategic planning and steps to success, we forget: life is not a business plan and the bottom line is not a number; formulas fail to factor in human foibles, and there is very little outside of ourselves that we actually *control.* Headlines of tsunamis, earthquakes and hurricanes remind us of this reality on a larger scale. In our personal lives, we chase the illusion—perhaps even more fiercely or frantically—that somehow we can, must or should be able to control what happens. With the best of intentions, we inform God of our agendas, ask His blessing and keep juggling, strategizing and manipulating in pathetic attempts to direct and produce outcomes for ourselves and our children.

My pastor friend Wayne takes it to another level: *God is not manageable.* He cannot be bargained with, manipulated, conned or cleverly outwitted. The little god in me would like to bump Him off the throne, and I do so on a daily basis, giving Him advice on how to answer my prayers; offering Him suggestions and strategies for outcomes; or worse, ignoring His promptings and doing life my way. I've noticed that God has not asked me to be His consultant, business manager or co-leader of the universe. He has it all nicely under control. Instead, He invites me to the relief of surrender. And when life tramples me down and piles on top of me, I finally give up and *reach up*, waving my white flag.

Today, instead of following my inclination to crawl under a rock, I sat on a dock by a small lake. The only movement was the soft, gentle breeze rippling across the surface of the water, reminding me that I must *be still* to notice the quiet movements of the Spirit in my life. "Be still, and know that I am God," He whispers through the psalmist (Psalm 46:10). The lake's glassy surface mirrored the vast, endless sky, the threshold of the universe where God effortlessly keeps the planets in their paths and governs unseen galaxies, reminding me that *He* is the One who holds *all* things together by the power of His Word. He's got everything under control; *every*thing . . . even the broken things. Holding life together does not depend on me after all; it depends on Him. Hallelujah! I just need to hand Him the reins and lean into Him. What a relief!

The unsettling, honest realization that life—and God—are unmanageable brings me to my knees at the foot of the cross, daily surrendering my willful desire to advise God how to run the world, or at least my little corner of it. The relief of letting go does not mean throwing caution to the wind or carelessly ignoring responsibility; it means throwing down my desire to control, and remembering who holds all the outcomes in His hands. This week, today, letting go means trusting that if God has permitted it, He will provide for it—the broken fridge, the car repair, a new watch. It means allowing Him to juggle my time to make room for His priorities and seeing my inconveniences as God's opportunities. It means trusting His voice to be more important than mine in my daughter's life, and biting my tongue so that she can hear Him.

At the foot of the cross, relinquishing control means remembering that His ways are not my ways and owning the words of Christ, "yet not my will, but yours be done" (Luke 22:42). Daily surrender is the path to freedom—receiving His life in me and allowing Him to live His life through me.

A Place of Surrender

*You turn things upside down, as if the potter were thought to be like the clay!
Shall what is formed say to him who formed it, "He did not make me"?
Can the pot say of the potter, "He knows nothing"?*
ISAIAH 29:16

*"My thoughts are nothing like your thoughts," says the LORD. "And my ways are
far beyond anything you could imagine. For just as the heavens are
higher than the earth, so my ways are higher than your ways and my
thoughts higher than your thoughts."*
ISAIAH 55:8-9, *NLT*

*Oh, the depth of the riches of the wisdom and knowledge of God!
How unsearchable his judgments, and his paths beyond tracing out! "Who has
known the mind of the Lord? Or who has been his counselor? Who has ever
given to God, that God should repay him?" For from him and through him
and to him are all things. To him be the glory forever! Amen.*
ROMANS 11:33-36

*All things were created by him and for him. He is before all things,
and in him all things hold together.*
COLOSSIANS 1:16-17

For Reflection

The serenity of surrendering life's outcomes keeps my relationship
with God in proper perspective, my emotions in proper check and my
priorities in proper order.

Living at a Place Near His Altar

When does life seem unmanageable to you?

What outcomes do you try to control?

What outcomes do you need to let go of today?

INVITING YOUR CHILDREN TO HIS ALTAR

With young children, play the game "Mother, May I?" Ask them why it is hard to ask, "Mother, may I?" What are the consequences if they do not ask? Relate this to the importance of yielding to God.

Ask your children to describe when they feel overwhelmed or out of control. What outcomes would they like to control?

Remind your children of Jesus' prayer in Gethsemane, "yet not my will, but yours be done" (Luke 22:42). Talk about Jesus' humanity; was it difficult for Jesus to surrender His will to His heavenly Father? What was the outcome when He did surrender?

PRAYER NOTES AND PERSONAL REFLECTIONS

A PLACE OF SURRENDER

Willing to Be Willing: The Path to Joy

Who in their right mind would want to listen to all this stuff every day? Slogging up the steps to my counselor's office, I couldn't imagine how wearisome it must be for a counselor to listen to clients wrestle in their mixed-up marriages day after day, week after week. *What a depressing vocation!*

Five years and one divorce later, I was wrestling with God, instead of my marriage. A lot of healing had taken place in me, and now it was time to get on with my life—but in what direction? The comfortable, convenient path—teaching Bible at my kids' Christian school—seemed cloistered. I sensed that following my creative interest in interior design wouldn't be ultimately satisfying. "Have you thought about going into counseling?" friends would suggest. Inwardly, I groaned, resisted and complained to God. *Please don't make me go down that road! Can't I just leave all that behind?* In a holy tug-of-war, I dug in my heels.

My friend Emily listened to my quandary with understanding and gently offered her feedback. "Carol, you have had a very unique journey. I don't think God took you down that road to teach junior-high Bible or decorate homes. I think He has a different purpose—to use your journey to help others traveling a similar path." I knew in my gut she was speaking truth to me and took her words to heart.

Emily brought her own unique perspective to the table: She was fighting a losing battle against cancer. She saw this life through a different lens, marking time. She lived intentionally, weighing the investment value of every opportunity. That conversation was my turning point of surrender. Instead of resisting, I began to be "willing to be willing."

Historically, people don't tend to cooperate easily when God communicates His plan. Spirit and flesh are like oil and water, so when

Spirit speaks, the flesh resists. Eve ate. Sarah laughed. Gideon hid. Moses questioned God and complained he wasn't up to the task. Jonah ran away. Peter argued. Ananias and Sapphira connived, to their own demise. None of these responses worked out well in the end. But the Bible also gives us better examples to follow—people who demonstrated a willingness to participate in God's revealed plan. Noah hammered it out. Abraham got up and went. Isaiah volunteered. Mary worshiped. Saul changed his name, and his direction. All of these individuals chose to live deliberately for the glory of God. By faith, they surrendered their own agendas, allowed God to turn their worlds upside down, and embarked on the journey of a lifetime.

Jesus, more than anyone else, empathizes with our struggle in surrender. In Gethsemene, He was "deeply troubled and distressed" and His soul was "crushed with grief to the point of death" (Mark 14:33-34, *NLT*). God's unfolding eternal plan, the cross, was imminent. Did Jesus struggle against the temptation to run, hide or choose a more convenient path? Yes; He was tempted in every way we are, and yet was without sin (see Hebrews 4:15). Twice, He desperately pled with His Father for an alternative plan; but twice, He was willing to be willing: "your will be done, not mine" (Matthew 26:39,42). Jesus knew that surrender was the path to true joy (see Hebrews 12:2).

Three weeks after our conversation, God took Emily unexpectedly; no one knew that her time was so short. I am so grateful she faithfully nudged me to a place of surrender—the place of being "willing to be willing." That turning point began an adventure of faith that has taken me through graduate school and into a counseling practice. Today, as I listen to my clients, I feel honored and humbled to have the opportunity to enter their complicated lives. In the center of my being, I know I am serving a holy purpose that is deeply satisfying and gives me joy. Crazy as it sounds, there is nothing I would rather be doing.

A PLACE OF SURRENDER

The eyes of the LORD search the whole earth in order to strengthen those whose hearts are fully committed to him.
2 CHRONICLES 16:9, *NLT*

Show me the right path, O LORD; point out the road for me to follow.
PSALM 25:4, NLT

*You have made known to me the path of life; you will fill me with joy in your
presence, with eternal pleasures at your right hand.*
PSALM 16:11

*The LORD will work out his plans for my life—for your faithful love,
O LORD, endures forever. Don't abandon me, for you made me.*
PSALM 138:8, NLT

"My food," said Jesus, "is to do the will of him who sent me and to finish his work."
JOHN 4:34

*For we do not have a high priest who is unable to sympathize with
our weaknesses, but we have one who has been tempted in every way,
just as we are—yet was without sin.*
HEBREWS 4:15

*Let us fix our eyes on Jesus, the author and perfecter of our faith,
who for the joy set before him endured the cross, scorning its shame,
and sat down at the right hand of the throne of God.*
HEBREWS 12:2

FOR REFLECTION

Surrender is the daily process of yielding. Surrender is not reluctantly
"giving in," as in being dragged across the line in a tug-of-war game,
but "giving over," as in letting go of the rope and stepping across the
line, pulling with God for His glory in our lives.

LIVING AT A PLACE OF SURRENDER

In what area of your life are you in a tug-of-war with God?

What would happen if you let go of the "rope," stepped over the line,
and started pulling with God?

How can you give God more "rope" in your life today?

INVITING YOUR CHILDREN TO A PLACE OF SURRENDER

Play tug-of-war with a few other families, (e.g., children vs. adults, boys vs. girls, families vs. families). Discuss how it felt during the struggle and how it felt to be on the losing or winning side. Relate the game to a way you have struggled with God.

Notice the role of power and control in battles you have with your children. Focus on winning their hearts rather than the particular battle at hand. Invite them to trust your love and wisdom when they have difficulty accepting the decisions you make.

Empower your children to make wise decisions by offering them God's "big picture" perspective. Encourage them to seek counsel from trusted adults and pray through their decision process. Let them own their decisions in age-appropriate ways.

PRAYER NOTES AND PERSONAL REFLECTIONS

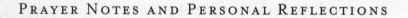

DAY 42

THE BATTLE OF SELF

Refusing to Rationalize

During recent weeks, my friendship with Ben had grown into a school-girl crush—my first genuine interest in a man in the many years since my divorce. We shared common religious, educational and geographical backgrounds; common interests; common losses; and common friends. I enjoyed his personality and was flattered by his pursuit. I was relieved when he suggested we discuss spiritual issues. This was one piece he had not shared very freely with me, and his oblique comments about theological questions had left me wondering if we were on the same page.

As Ben shared his spiritual journey, I felt my heart sink under the weight of his words. Although I did not have the expectation that Ben and I would necessarily be in the same place spiritually, I was unprepared for the discovery of how very far apart we were. How could I experience spiritual intimacy with someone who had shelved his Bible years ago, questioning its relevance to his everyday life? How could I love and serve Christ wholeheartedly yet be emotionally entangled with someone who seemed ambivalent?

"Ben, I'm running a race. I need to be with someone who will encourage my faith when I struggle and take me back to the Word when I veer off course," I explained. Although I spoke with resolve, Ben had wriggled past the deadbolt of my heart. It was both startling and disturbing to admit my vulnerability as I heard the voice of self-gratification whispering rationalizations.

Esau knew the temptation of self-gratification (see Genesis 25). This man was hungry! The aroma from the meal Jacob served up made his nostrils curl. Man, that smelled good! Desire made Esau nearsighted, even myopic. All he saw was the opportunity to get his hunger satisfied. Perhaps he rationalized or even blamed God for his predicament. *It's natural to be hungry; surely God doesn't expect me to live with a growling stomach!* Driven by desire, he bartered the blessing of his father and his birthright as the firstborn son for a bowl of Jacob's stew. What a costly compote! Esau bet the whole farm, thinking it wouldn't make a difference, or not thinking at all. It never dawned on Esau that his immediate gratification would result in long-term personal and relational losses. He had no way of knowing that his compromise would ultimately impact generations to come.

Like Esau, we face powerful, daily temptations to meet our own needs in our own way, at the cost of forfeiting God's joy and blessing in our life. We, too, can be shortsighted, often having no way of fore-seeing the long-term consequences of our rationalizations. We're tempted to bet the farm, thinking it won't matter or that our way is better than God's, or not thinking at all. Alternatively, God invites us to believe that His good gifts are far better than any good we might grasp for ourselves, and to trust Him to satisfy our desires in His way and in His time. Jesus modeled this for us during His temptation in the wilderness, in Gethsemene and, ultimately, on the cross. He showed us that resisting self-gratification wasn't easy and wasn't with-out cost; but it was the path to true life and joy.

Each day, we make choices to surrender—either to self or to God. Surrendering to God means resisting the temptation to rationalize, refusing self-serving strategies and rejecting compromise. It means betting that God knows better than we do. Surrender means giving up self to the One who gave Himself up for us on the cross, the ulti-mate expression of His willingness to go the distance to give us God's best. Surrender means yielding our desires to a good and faithful God, trusting God-given boundaries as a loving expression of His wisdom, and relying on His unfailing love to have our best interests at heart.

Relinquishing my relationship with Ben was not easy, but it was clearly a necessary choice, honoring Ben's journey and my integrity. Sur-render meant changing the course of a valuable relationship in order to stay the course in the one relationship that is invaluable. It meant standing my ground at the foot of the cross, believing that if God has a life partner for me, our paths will cross there—each of us surrendered to God's love and both of us loving God through surrendered living.

A PLACE OF SURRENDER

Take delight in the Lord, and he will give you your heart's desires.
Commit everything you do to the Lord. Trust him, and he will help you.
PSALM 37:4-5, *NLT*

My people have committed two sins: They have forsaken me,
the spring of living water, and have dug their own cisterns,
broken cisterns that cannot hold water.
JEREMIAH 2:13

After fasting forty days and forty nights, he was hungry. The tempter came
to him and said, "If you are the Son of God, tell these stones to become bread."
Jesus answered, "It is written: 'Man does not live on bread alone, but on every
word that comes from the mouth of God.'"
MATTHEW 4:2-4

Then he said to them all: "If anyone would come after me, he must deny
himself and take up his cross daily and follow me. For whoever wants to save
his life will lose it, but whoever loses his life for me will save it. What good is it
for a man to gain the whole world, and yet lose or forfeit his very self?"
LUKE: 9:23-25

FOR REFLECTION

"He is no fool who gives up what he cannot keep to gain what he cannot lose." —Jim Elliot, martyred missionary

LIVING AT A PLACE NEAR HIS ALTAR

How does the voice of self-gratification tempt you?

Ask God to examine your thoughts; what choices do you rationalize?

What would it mean to surrender this area to God?

INVITING YOUR CHILDREN TO HIS ALTAR

Empathize with your children when they struggle to obey; identify similar struggles you had at their age. Remind them that learning to submit to you teaches them how to submit to other authority figures in their lives, and ultimately, to God.

Help your children recognize when self-gratification and rationalization are influencing their choices.

It may not seem like your children are noticing, but they are watching in front-row seats; your life is their instruction manual. How do they see you living in surrender to God's purposes?

PRAYER NOTES AND PERSONAL REFLECTIONS

WORRY

God's Supply Is Sufficient

Walking through the crowded, insect-infested outdoor market, I felt conspicuously white, Western and wealthy. I was in Burundi, Africa, one of the smallest and poorest countries of the world, where people quietly struggle for life one day at a time. With the help of a translator, some young widows gratefully related how the mission agency's micro-loan enabled them to start a small business milling casaba flour, which provided enough meager income to sustain their families. A motherless teenage girl, taking my measurements for a *kitenge,* enthusiastically shared how her sewing machine, also purchased through a micro-loan, enabled her to support her invalid father and her siblings. Remembering my last-minute fretting and shopping for items I "needed" before my trip, I felt rebuked by the joy and simple contentment of these Burundian women. They had no expectation of ease or entitlement, and no self-pity. Instead, they lived in the moment with acceptance and faithful dependence on God. They reminded me of another poor widow, a single mom in the Old Testament who learned to rely on God as her Provider, one day at a time.

Under the rule of self-serving kings, the Israelites had wandered far from God; idolatry was rampant in the land. A drought was God's judgment on His people for trusting in other gods. Would those other gods feed Israel? But God told His servant Elijah to go to the brook of Kerith: "You will drink from the brook, and I have ordered the ravens to feed you there" (1 Kings 17:4). This was an unusual command and an odd arrangement, but Elijah obeyed and experienced God's extraordinary provision when he was fed by the birds day after day. Eventually, the brook dried up, but not God's provision. He told Elijah to go to Zarephath, where He had commanded a non-Israelite widow to feed Elijah—another unusual command, another odd arrangement. Shouldn't the man of God be providing food for the widow instead?

But even as the birds had fed Elijah, his faith in Jehovah-jireh—the Provider-God who keeps His Word—had been strengthened. So Elijah set out to find the widow.

Life for the widow had turned from desolate to desperate. When Elijah came begging for bread, she gave him the bare facts: she was down to her very last ounce of flour and oil. She and her son would have one last meal and die. She had nothing but crumbs; Elijah had nothing but God. She knew her circumstances, but Elijah knew Jehovah-jireh. "Don't be afraid" he coaxed, knowing that fear pulls the plug on faith. "If you trust God and share what you have with me, God will provide you with enough. Enough for today, and enough to keep sharing until the end of the drought" (see 1 Kings 17:13-14).

With nothing to lose and everything to gain, the widow borrowed an ounce of Elijah's faith, mixed it with her ounce of flour and oil and took a gamble on the God of Israel. Her initial faith experiment became a daily faith experience. Taking God at His Word and stepping out in unreasonable obedience, she experienced God's extraordinary provision day after day!

But in time, her son became ill and died. Losing her only son, she lost her hope as well; now who would care for her in old age? It seemed God had abandoned her after all. But Elijah prayed, and the life-giving, life-sustaining Provider-God of Israel brought the son back to life, showing the non-Israelite widow that God alone was the faithful Source of *every* present and future provision in her life. With each provision, He proved His sufficiency. Eventually, seeing became believing; God alone was her hope.

God provides through ordinary as well as extraordinary means. His unusual provisions remind us that He has means beyond the scope of our knowledge and understanding. His most extravagant provision was at the cross. "For God so loved the world that he *gave* his one and only Son . . ." (John 3:16, emphasis mine). In Christ, God became both the Provider and the Provision, the Giver and the Gift.

Out of love, God gave of Himself without measure; He continues to give Himself to all who will rely on Him. Whether we are down to our last dollar, last ounce of energy, last shred of patience or last kernel of faith—when we choose to depend on Him, He will provide. God is Jehovah-jireh, and He will keep His Word.

A Place of Celebrating God's Provision

The eyes of all look to you in hope; you give them their food as they need it. When
you open your hand, you satisfy the hunger and thirst of every living thing.
PSALM 145:15-16, *NLT*

That is why I tell you not to worry about everyday life—whether you
have enough food and drink, or enough clothes to wear. Isn't life more
than food, and your body more than clothing? . . . Can all your worries
add a single moment to your life? . . . So don't worry about these things,
saying, "What will we eat? What will we drink? What will we wear?"
These things dominate the thoughts of unbelievers, but your heavenly
Father already knows all your needs. Seek the Kingdom of God above all else,
and live righteously, and he will give you everything you need.
MATTHEW 6:25,27,31-33, *NLT*

Don't worry about anything; instead, pray about everything.
Tell God what you need, and thank him for all he has done. Then you will
experience God's peace, which exceeds anything we can understand.
His peace will guard your hearts and minds as you live in Christ Jesus.
PHILIPPIANS 4:6-7, *NLT*

For Reflection

Our needs are God's opportunities; we were created to live in dependence on Him, not independent of Him!

Living at a Place Near His Altar

In what ways are you inclined to rely on yourself instead of on God?

What do you lack today? Is this lack a "want" or a "need"?

Is God prompting you to take a step of faith or obedience as you rely on Him?

INVITING YOUR CHILDREN TO HIS ALTAR

Watch television commercials with your children; discuss the difference between "needs" and "wants."

Pray with your children about their concerns; remind them that sometimes God says yes, sometimes no, and sometimes He tells us to wait. Sometimes He provides in unexpected, unimagined ways!

Children often take daily provisions for granted. Consider opening their eyes by volunteering as a family at a local food pantry or a ministry that feeds the homeless.

PRAYER NOTES AND PERSONAL REFLECTIONS

_____
_____
_____
_____
_____
_____
_____
_____
_____
_____
_____
_____
_____
_____
_____
_____
_____
_____
_____

DAY 44

DEPENDENCE

God Is in the Details

When my divorce was finalized, I was granted permission to move with my children to Texas. I felt relieved and also overwhelmed by the size of the task before me. I had two months to sell our house, buy a house, do a massive garage sale, pack up all our belongings and tie up miscellaneous loose ends—with a long string of tearful farewells woven into the emotional mix. How would everything get done? "First things first" and "one day at a time" became my new mantras; plans were swept along by an undercurrent of prayer, asking God to provide for every detail. If I had listened hard, I might have heard some muffled laughter from behind the curtain of heaven. Little did I know the rapid succession of surprises God had in store over the next three weeks!

Ten days later, we headed to Dallas on a house-hunting expedition. *Lord, You said "I go to prepare a place for you"; I'm counting on it!* For three days, we looked at dozens of houses, but through unusual circumstances God provided a home for us that wasn't even on the market! It was in move-in condition, recently remodeled and updated, and each of the rooms was already painted in our personal color preferences. To our surprise, the bedroom that would be Robin's room even held a bedroom set identical to her own!

God's fingerprints were everywhere, but He wasn't finished providing. After returning home, I learned that a newly hired church pastor would be house-hunting in the area that week. I worked frantically to put my home in order and hired a "random" college student to do desperately needed yard work. Upon learning his parents were missionaries in the Dallas area, I also hired him to drive our van and dog to Dallas, and I smiled at God's mysterious ways. A few minutes later,

I laughed incredulously when the same "random" yard guy informed me that his other summer job was working for a moving company! Within two days, I had a moving bid and my garage was filled with free boxes provided by his company.

God was blowing me kisses, but He still wasn't finished providing. My sister and a friend helped put finishing touches on my house; the next day I sold it to the new pastor without ever listing it. I imagine God was grinning like an amused parent on Christmas morning. *God was in the details—all of them.* It had been exactly three weeks since my divorce; miraculously, I still had five weeks left—to pack, have a garage sale, say farewells and go! My head was spinning in the whirlwind, but God was in the calm center, confirming that I could depend on Him as my Provider.

When Moses stepped into God's plan to lead the Israelites out of Egypt, he didn't know how God would accomplish it. Parting the Red Sea? Manna from heaven? Quail ad nauseum? Water from a rock? God rarely provides us with the details in advance; if He did, we wouldn't believe it! Instead God provides us with His promises and puts Himself up as collateral. He is Jehovah-jireh, our Provider. His Name is His guarantee.

Ultimately, our Jehovah-jireh put Himself on the cross to be our Provider not only for this life but also for the life to come—an amazing plan He mapped out before the foundation of the world. At the foot of the cross, He went the distance from heaven to hell to be our Provider. We can surely trust Him for the details of today.

A PLACE OF PROVISION

Commit everything you do to the Lord. Trust him, and he will help you. . . .
The Lord directs the steps of the godly. He delights in every detail of their lives.
Though they stumble, they will never fall, for the Lord holds them by the hand.
PSALM 37:5,23-24, *NLT*

Trust in the LORD with all your heart; do not depend on your own understanding.
Seek his will in all you do, and he will show you which path to take.
PROVERBS 3:5-6, *NLT*

They did not thirst when he led them through the deserts; he made water
flow for them from the rock; he split the rock and water gushed out.
ISAIAH 48:21

And God will generously provide all you need. Then you will always have
everything you need and plenty left over to share with others.
2 CORINTHIANS 9:8, *NLT*

Because of the sacrifice of the Messiah, his blood poured out on the
altar of the Cross, we're a free people—free of penalties and punishments
chalked up by all our misdeeds. And not just barely free, either.
Abundantly free! He thought of everything, provided for everything we could
possibly need, letting us in on the plans he took such delight in
making. He set it all out before us in Christ, a long-range plan in which
everything would be brought together and summed up in him,
everything in deepest heaven, everything on planet earth.
EPHESIANS 1:7, *THE MESSAGE*

And this same God who takes care of me will supply all your needs from
his glorious riches, which have been given to us in Christ Jesus.
PHILIPPIANS 4:19, *NLT*

FOR REFLECTION

Where God gives vision, He makes provision. His fingerprints are in
the details.

LIVING AT A PLACE NEAR HIS ALTAR

When is it most difficult for you to trust God as your Provider?

What do you need to let go of in order to rely on God?

How does "first things first" and "one day at a time" challenge your
dependence on God?

INVITING YOUR CHILDREN TO HIS ALTAR

Read the story of the Exodus from Egypt (see Exodus 12-18). Make a list of the many ways God provided for His people. How has He provided for your family?

Relate the advance preparations you made for your child's birth. Remind your children that they are precious to God and how much more than any earthly parent He lovingly prepares and provides for all they need!

Invite your children to become God-detectives, looking for God's answers to prayer, and noticing His "fingerprints" in the details!

PRAYER NOTES AND PERSONAL REFLECTIONS

_____
_____
_____
_____
_____
_____
_____
_____
_____
_____
_____
_____
_____
_____
_____
_____
_____
_____
_____

REST

God Is Enough

"My kids come first; work is a close second." This is how the priorities of single moms usually line up: who you love the most, what you need the most. We give and give to keep those two areas covered, and at the end of the day, we hope we've given enough. *How much is enough?* Enough so that our kids feel loved and our employers value us enough to keep us on the payroll. Enough to feel okay about ourselves—that we measure up to some undefined bar that eludes our reach. Enough to assuage the gut feeling that what we give may never actually be quite enough, especially where our kids are concerned. Tomorrow we will try again; tomorrow night we will wonder again.

Love and need are powerful motivators, prompting us to give more and do more until we are chasing our tails 24/7. Like Pavlov's dogs, we modify our behavior so that we continue to receive validation that enough is enough—or perhaps that *we* are enough. This is where we become vulnerable. *In our twisted, frenetic world, it's easy to forget that life does not really revolve around our kids or our work.* Caught up in the melee, we forget where true life is found.

God prefaced the Ten Commandments with this reminder: "I am the LORD your God, who brought you out of Egypt, out of the land of slavery" (Exodus 20:2). *Don't forget Me, and don't forget I'm inviting you to a new way of living!* The first three commands reveal God's jealous love, His longing for the hearts of His chosen people to be devoted wholly to Himself. But they reverted to tangible idols—to little gods they could grasp, manipulate and appease that gave them the false sense they could control life rather than rely on God as the Source and Provider of life.

The fourth command, to observe the Sabbath and keep it holy, challenged their self-reliance. Every seventh day, the rhythm of life was intentionally interrupted; work came to a screeching halt. "Enough!" Sabbath rest provided a much-needed reminder that they were not supernaturally self-sufficient, but humanly God-dependent. Work is good and serves worthwhile purposes, but the command to *stop* work keeps it in perspective; God is our Source of life and our Provider in life. Everything revolves around Him—even our work.

"You have six days each week for your ordinary work, but on the seventh day you must stop working, even during the seasons of plowing and harvest" (Exodus 34:21, *NLT*). That last phrase is hard to swallow; how easily we rationalize longer hours and life without margins during work-intensive seasons. Sadly, those seasons tend to merge into one another. *I'll be able to work less when . . . I just need to get past this deadline . . . After this project is done . . .* We compare notes on the intensity of our schedules—how much we pack into our days or weeks to be all things to all people—as if comparing badges of significance. This is a clue that our compass has gone haywire. Sabbath rest reorients us to our true north. Jesus reminded the Pharisees that the Sabbath was God's provision for man. God's call to Sabbath rest honors the limitations of our humanity.

Sabbath rest reminds me that I am not God; everything does not depend on me, but on Him. He is the Provider, even in "seasons of plowing and harvest."

As single moms, we need to get off the merry-go-round to remember that our truest need is for God Himself. God declared the seventh day holy ("set apart"); it was the day He rested from all His work and delighted in His creation (see Genesis 2:3). We, too, are called to rest from our work and delight in our Creator. "Enough is enough!"—not because we have done enough, but because God is Enough. Through rest and worship, our hearts are reordered, our perspective is renewed and our bodies refreshed.

At the cross, Jesus said, "It is finished!" His unconditional love bridged the gap between us and God, created by sin and shame—putting an end to our striving to be and do enough. The Provider and Sustainer of life gave up His life to give us new life. At the foot of the cross, we realize that then and now, He is our Sufficiency. He is Enough.

A PLACE OF PROVISION

*Observe the Sabbath day, to keep it holy. Work six days and do everything you
need to do. But the seventh day is a Sabbath to God, your God. Don't do any
work—not you, nor your son, nor your daughter, nor your servant, nor your
maid, nor your animals, not even the foreign guest visiting in your town. For in six
days God made Heaven, Earth, and sea, and everything in them; he rested on the
seventh day. Therefore God blessed the Sabbath day; he set it apart as a holy day.*
EXODUS 20:8-11, *THE MESSAGE*

*Say to the Israelites, "You must observe my Sabbaths. This will be a
sign between me and you for the generations to come, so you may know
that I am the LORD, who makes you holy."*
EXODUS 31:13

*This is what the Sovereign LORD, the Holy One of Israel, says: "Only in
returning to me and resting in me will you be saved. In quietness and confidence
is your strength. But you would have none of it."*
ISAIAH 30:15, *NLT*

*Then Jesus said to them, "The Sabbath was made to meet the needs of people,
and not people to meet the requirements of the Sabbath."*
MARK 2:27, *NLT*

FOR REFLECTION

Rest reminds us that God is the Provider of our significance.

LIVING AT A PLACE NEAR HIS ALTAR

What priorities do your children observe in your life?

Why is rest important, even in your busiest seasons?

What boundaries would help you honor the Sabbath and create pockets
of rest in your schedule?

INVITING YOUR CHILDREN TO HIS ALTAR

Discuss the benefits of rest with your children: health, productivity, positive attitudes, alert minds. What margins of rest are in your children's lives?

Identify ways to "set apart" Sunday to worship God and be refreshed. Set apart time on the family calendar for these activities.

Work hard, play hard. Affirm the importance of work and play—both are gifts from God!

PRAYER NOTES AND PERSONAL REFLECTIONS

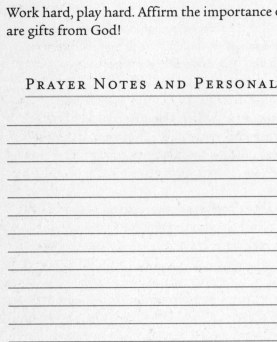

RELIANCE

The Pathway to Thanksgiving

Last week, my friend Pam hauled two kids to the ER—different days, different events—to the tune of over $1,000. In recent weeks, her car was vandalized, her ceiling fan caught fire and her daughter's close friend died. Over the past few months, her promising new job has failed to deliver on its promises, and her daughter's father has failed to deliver on his financial promises as well. Each week, it seems as if Pam gets slammed by people and circumstances beyond her control. She lives pressed between the crushing margins of time, money, energy and family concerns.

Nevertheless, Pam maintains a hopeful attitude around her children. Her outlook is neither "Pollyanna pretending" nor "Little Orphan Annie optimism"; Pam faces grim realities in her life head-on. But she is a fighter; every time life knocks her down, Pam lands on her knees and does battle in prayer. Underneath Pam's quick smile and gentle laughter is an attitude of gratitude for the ways she continually sees God at work in the midst of her overwhelming circumstances. For this reason, Pam is my heroine of single moms.

When life happens to us, and circumstances rob us of our choice and our voice, the powerlessness we feel can lead to discouragement, despair and a victim mentality. Pam chooses not to embrace that identity or get stuck there; that would give too much power and control to people and circumstances in her life. Instead, she chooses to embrace her identity as a child of God, claim the promises of God and rely on God's power and control in her unpredictable life circumstances. *No matter what happens*, Pam entrusts herself and her children to God, confident that He has the upper hand. On her knees in dependence, Pam has found a vantage point to see the big picture, producing courage, resilience and a thankful heart.

Paul operated from the same vantage point. In return for preaching the gospel, he endured beatings, imprisonment, shipwreck and two years of house arrest. During his house arrest, he could have worn the label "victim" and thrown a pity party. Instead, he entrusted his circumstances to God, devoted himself to prayer and wrote hope-filled letters to encourage other believers. His letter to the Colossians starts with thanksgiving, then launches into a magnificent liturgy on the supremacy of Christ and the sovereignty of God. Only at the very end of the letter does Paul even mention his circumstances. Likewise, his letter to the Philippians is characterized by thanksgiving, joy and hope. Paul's reliance on the sovereignty and goodness of God was the cornerstone of his humility, enabled him to see beyond his circumstances, and produced an attitude of gratitude.

On the eve of His crucifixion, with the "big picture" in view, Jesus gave thanks as He broke the bread and poured the wine, representing His body that would be broken and His blood that would be shed for our sin. Jesus chose not to be a victim of people or circumstances; even on the cross, He entrusted Himself to the God who is completely in control (see Luke 23:46, *NLT*). In His life and in His death, Jesus chose humility over pride and dependence over power.

Pam doesn't overcome her circumstances by pulling herself up by her own worn-out bootstraps; they could never withstand the weight of the burdens she carries. Instead, Pam tenaciously pushes through life empowered by the counter-intuitive choice to be dependent. The discipline of dependence has produced an attitude of gratitude; Pam counts on God and counts her blessings.

A PLACE OF THANKSGIVING

We were crushed and overwhelmed beyond our ability to endure, and we thought we would never live through it. In fact, we expected to die. But as a result, we stopped relying on ourselves and learned to rely only on God, who raises the dead. And he did rescue us from mortal danger, and he will rescue us again. We have placed our confidence in him, and he will continue to rescue us.

And you are helping us by praying for us. Then many people will give thanks
because God has graciously answered so many prayers for our safety.
2 CORINTHIANS 1:8-11, *NLT*

So I wouldn't get a big head, I was given the gift of a handicap
to keep me in constant touch with my limitations. Satan's angel did his
best to get me down; what he in fact did was push me to my knees.
No danger then of walking around high and mighty! At first I didn't
think of it as a gift, and begged God to remove it. Three times I did that,
and then he told me, "My grace is enough; it's all you need. My strength
comes into its own in your weakness." Once I heard that, I was glad to let it hap-
pen. I quit focusing on the handicap and began appreciating the gift.
It was a case of Christ's strength moving in on my weakness. Now I take
limitations in stride, and with good cheer, these limitations that cut me
down to size—abuse, accidents, opposition, bad breaks. I just let
Christ take over! And so the weaker I get, the stronger I become.
2 CORINTHIANS 12:7-10, *THE MESSAGE*

Devote yourselves to prayer with an alert mind and a thankful heart.
COLOSSIANS 4:2, *NLT*

FOR REFLECTION

Self-reliance produces pride; God-reliance produces thanksgiving.

LIVING AT A PLACE NEAR HIS ALTAR

How do the labels "victim" and "overcomer" affect your view of your-self and your situation?

What promises has God given you that help you see beyond your current circumstances?

What are you relying on God for today? What are some blessings you can thank God for today?

INVITING YOUR CHILDREN TO HIS ALTAR

Read your children the Bible stories of Joseph, Daniel and Paul. What were the attitudes of these men when they were "victims"? How did God bring good out of their circumstances?

Children gain a big-picture view from the stories of our lives. Describe a time when you had to rely on God. What could you have been thankful for at the time? How do you view that situation now?

Life's obstacles are God's opportunities; sympathize with your children's disappointments and difficulties, but avoid their "pity parties." Instead, pray with them about the situation—acknowledging God's control in all things, relying on His character and thanking Him for His sufficiency.

PRAYER NOTES AND PERSONAL REFLECTIONS

PRAISE

Choosing an Attitude of Gratitude

"Where did you get your sign?" I asked the cashier at the local grocery store. It read, "Attitude Is Everything." I could tell this cashier believed it and lived it. Her cheerful attitude was contagious—a blessing to everyone who came through her lane. I needed her attitude far more than I needed any of the items I was purchasing that day. Before leaving the store, I made a copy of her sign on the store copy machine.

For years, that sign was taped to my bathroom mirror, serving as a daily reminder to me and my kids that we are responsible for our attitudes and that our attitudes influence our "response-ability" as we navigate the circumstances of life. Whether dealing with a difficult situation at school or correcting a less-than-desirable attitude toward me, I reminded by kids, "There's a lot you don't get to choose in life, *but you do get to choose your attitude!*" And always, I was challenged by my own words.

Today, those words brought me under conviction again when a home repairman presented me with an unexpected estimate of $500. As we calmly discussed the necessary repair and my options, I felt myself reacting internally—stomach knotting, muscles tensing, my morning headache returning. Life's unpleasant surprises are my triggers to grumble, gripe and growl; platitudes about attitudes can be quickly forgotten. But then Paul's familiar words in Philippians 4:5-7 gently knocked on the back door of my mind: "Let your gentleness be evident to all. The Lord is near. Do not be anxious about anything, but in everything, by prayer and petition, with thanksgiving, present your requests to God. And the peace of God, which transcends all understanding, will guard your hearts and your minds in Christ Jesus." The

Spirit paraphrased: *Don't growl at anyone. The all-sufficient, sovereign God is present in this surprise situation. Nothing has escaped His notice. Talk to Him; thank Him for His sovereignty and sufficiency! Let Him give you supernatural peace. Fretting won't help; God will!*

As I mulled over Paul's words, the Spirit talked me down off my ledge of anxiety. These were the words of someone who invited the power of the Indwelling Spirit to govern his internal reactions and responses to external circumstances beyond his control. Two key words, "with thanksgiving," are at the very center of this passage about anxiety. They seem oddly placed; we usually say "thank you" when someone hands us something desirable, not when we are handed a bag of rocks! But from his Jewish theology, Paul understood the sovereignty of God. *All* of life is under God's control; our lives are solidly, securely in God's hands. His fingers faithfully filter whatever bundle of trouble He allows to touch our lives, and in that circumstance, He gives Himself over to us as The One Who Is All-Sufficient.

Paul neatly centered the phrase "with thanksgiving" in the sandwich of prayers, petitions and requests we present to God, because in giving thanks, we acknowledge our dependence on the Giver. God does not take advantage of our dependence, but views it as something precious and valuable. Knowing that we need protection from the clamoring paparazzi of fear and worry, He assigns a watchful guard, "the peace of God," to be our escort, buffering us through the circumstances of the day.

At the foot of the cross, we remember Jesus' perfect example of trust in the sovereignty of God. Throughout His betrayal, trial, torture and crucifixion, Jesus' attitudes were governed by the Spirit—even under the most extreme physical and emotional stress. Rather than reacting to men or circumstances, the Prince of Peace entrusted Himself to God the Father and offered mercy to His offenders. Rather than using His power to control others, He exercised self-control, knowing that His Father God was *completely* in control. "Be anxious for nothing."

Today, as I reviewed my checkbook and calculated my home repair bill, I got to choose—not only which repair option was preferable but also which attitude was preferable. By the grace of God, I chose an attitude of gratitude.

A PLACE OF THANKSGIVING

The Lord is my strength and my shield; my heart trusts in him, and I am helped.
My heart leaps for joy and I will give thanks to him in song.
PSALM 28:7

Make thankfulness your sacrifice to God, and keep the vows you
made to the Most High. Then call on me when you are in trouble,
and I will rescue you, and you will give me glory.
PSALM 50:14-15, *NLT*

It is good to give thanks to the LORD, to sing praises to the Most High.
It is good to proclaim your unfailing love in the morning,
your faithfulness in the evening.
PSALM 92:1-2, *NLT*

Let your roots grow down into him, and let your lives be built on him.
Then your faith will grow strong in the truth you were taught,
and you will overflow with thankfulness.
COLOSSIANS 2:7, *NLT*

Be cheerful no matter what; pray all the time; thank God no matter what
happens. This is the way God wants you who belong to Christ Jesus to live.
1 THESSALONIANS 5:16-18, *THE MESSAGE*

FOR REFLECTION

I may not get to choose my circumstances, but I can always choose my attitudes and my reactions.

LIVING AT A PLACE NEAR HIS ALTAR

What example do your attitudes set for your children?

What situations are your "triggers" to grumble, gripe and growl? Make an "Attitude Is Everything" reminder for yourself, inviting Christ to rule in those situations.

A disciple is one who is "disciplined" in following Christ. How can you cultivate the discipline of thanksgiving?

INVITING YOUR CHILDREN TO HIS ALTAR

Discuss the phrase "Attitude Is Everything." How do good or bad attitudes influence situations on the playground, at school or in sports? Encourage your children to set the pace among their peers with good attitudes, pointing others to Christ.

To nurture attitudes of gratitude, play the "Gratitude Game." The goal is to outdo one another in gratitude throughout the course of a day. Celebrate at the end of the day by expressing ways you are thankful for one another.

Thanksgiving Day can be any day! Consider cooking a turkey dinner quarterly. Read a psalm of thanksgiving and encourage each child to identify what he or she is thankful for. Create a family "thanksgiving journal" that you keep throughout the year.

PRAYER NOTES AND PERSONAL REFLECTIONS

_____

_____

_____

_____

_____

_____

_____

_____

_____

_____

_____

_____

_____

DAILY EVENTS

Giving Thanks in All Circumstances

Hurricane Ike's devastation of the Texas coastline was mind-boggling; it looked like a war zone. Over a million residents evacuated, scrambling for their lives. Thousands arrived at the Dallas Convention Center with only the clothes on their backs and whatever belongings they could carry. Many people had no homes or businesses to return to; the "lucky" ones faced the clean-up work of significant damage caused by flooding and severe winds. At the Convention Center, a reporter thrust a microphone in front of a middle-aged woman, asking how she was managing. "I'm just so thankful," she said with a broad smile, her eyes sparkling. The startled reporter stuttered in response, rephrasing the same question. The woman replied again, "I'm just so thankful to have a roof over my head and a place to sleep, and all these caring people who are helping us; everyone has been wonderful. Sure, I'd like to go home, but I'm so grateful to be here." What kind of heart is thankful in the face of such horrible circumstances? Her words of gratitude were like the refreshing breezes left in Ike's wake.

When I was growing up, my father offered the same prayer every evening at dinner time: "Gracious heavenly Father, we thank Thee again for Thy goodness to us, and for all Thy care over us. We thank Thee for this food Thou hast provided, and we ask Thy blessing on it, in Jesus' precious name, Amen." As a child, Dad's prayer was so ingrained in my experience, I hardly paid attention to the words—except for noticing they were *always* the same. This was significant, because my spiritual tradition discouraged any kind of rote or memorized prayers. But every night at dinnertime, Dad offered the same soothing, rhythmic words.

Years later, as an adult, I came to appreciate Dad's constancy. Circumstances didn't alter his attitude of thanksgiving. A bad day at the office, a conflict at home, the inconvenience of a broken-down car or concerns about the rising cost of living—day after day, year after year, Dad thanked God for His goodness to us, His care over us and the basic provision of daily food. It was that simple.

Life changes, God doesn't. Bad things happen; God is still good and is still caring for us. Day in and day out, God is on the Throne.

At the Passover supper—celebrating and remembering the fulfillment of God's promise to deliver His people from 430 years of oppression and slavery in Egypt, Jesus also gave thanks. In this Passover supper, Jesus gave new meaning to the traditional bread and wine of the Passover feast. He revealed Himself as the sacrificial Passover Lamb provided by God, the fulfillment of God's promise to deliver people from the bondage of sin. From now on, the bread and wine of this supper would represent His body and blood. Ever since, the Lord's Supper has been celebrated among Christians as the Eucharist—a term meaning "thanksgiving."

How could Jesus give thanks as He faced betrayal, suffering and crucifixion? Perhaps He gave thanks because His Father was still on the Throne, still in control. Perhaps He was looking forward to what God would do: thankful that through His death, people would be given eternal life instead of judgment; thanking God that He would be faithful to raise Jesus from the dead; thanking God as He anticipated celebrating this feast again in His new Kingdom. All we know is that on the eve of His impending crucifixion, Jesus lifted His eyes above His circumstances and gave thanks to God—the God who is in control; the God who keeps His promises and delivers His people; the God of unfailing love and faithfulness.

And isn't that exactly why we give thanks in all circumstances, *especially* in difficulties? When the winds blow and the storms come, and the very doorstep of our life is washed away, that is precisely when we can thankfully remember that there is One who sits on the Throne, who keeps His promises and intervenes on our behalf. We thank God for who He is because He is good and His faithful love endures, day by day. In the storms of life, we throw our anchor in this truth at the foot of the cross and give thanks, praying, *Jesus, be formed in me.*

A Place of Thanksgiving

Give thanks to the Lord, for he is good. His love endures forever . . .
to him who alone does great wonders, His love endures forever.
who by his understanding made the heavens, His love endures forever.
who spread out the earth upon the waters, His love endures forever . . . .
to the One who remembered us in our low estate, His love endures forever.
and freed us from our enemies, His love endures forever.
and who gives food to every creature. His love endures forever.
Give thanks to the God of heaven. His love endures forever.
PSALM 136:1,4-6,23-26

For Reflection

Jesus affirmed the severe reality of life's heartaches, difficulties and disappointments, and He promised Himself as our Overcomer: "I have told you all this so that you may have peace in me. Here on earth you will have many trials and sorrows. But take heart, because I have overcome the world" (John 16:33, *NLT*). For this, we give thanks!

Living at a Place Near His Altar

What can you thank God for in the midst of a current storm in your life?

How does your knowledge of God's goodness and unfailing love cultivate a thankful heart?

How frequently do you celebrate the Lord's Supper—the Eucharist—with other believers?

Inviting Your Children to His Altar

Be on the lookout for your kids' good attitudes. Take time to appreciate a job well done and kindnesses they show each other. What can you thank your children for today?

Read Psalm 136 in its entirety. In the same pattern, write a family psalm relating God's activity in your family's story; repeat "His love endures forever" in each stanza.

At dinnertime, play the "Alphabet Game"; going around the table, each person thinks of something to be thankful for, starting with each letter of the alphabet.

PRAYER NOTES AND PERSONAL REFLECTIONS

_____
_____
_____
_____
_____
_____
_____
_____
_____
_____
_____
_____
_____
_____
_____
_____
_____
_____
_____
_____
_____
_____
_____
_____
_____

DESPAIR

Finding Handholds in the Dark

In Illinois, winter arrived early and overstayed her welcome. The relentless winter arrived in late October and dragged on until late April. By January, "winter darkness" would creep over me, a heaviness of spirit matching the heavy gray winter clouds blocking my view of the sun. Groundhog Day became an all-important "national holiday" to me. Would Punxsutawny Phil predict that spring would come early or late? I *hoped* it would be early.

What does the winter of your life look like? Perhaps it is an interminable season of wrestling with the wills of toddlers or teenagers, and you are battle-weary. Maybe you are grieving a relational loss or you are unhappy being single, longing for the companionship of a life partner. Your personal winter might be financial (unreliable child support, the loss of a job or loss of economic security) or situational (a difficult boss or coworker, or a dead-end job). Perhaps your winter darkness is characterized by depression or the emotional struggles of sorting out a painful past. Perhaps your winter is spiritual—the darkness of doubt, the battle to believe in the goodness of God, or shaken confidence in His love.

In our personal winters, the shadows of life loom long and large, and our questions and struggles about God, ourselves and life loom even larger. We wait and hope to turn the corner into spring, but we don't know when it will come, and there is no "ground hog prediction" to give us hope. Hope is what we grope for and hold on to in the dark, if we can find it. But what is hope?

Biblical hope is *not* "Pollyanna pretending" that things are better than they are. In this stance we are quick to brush away tears, minimize, spiritualize or theologize about life's disappointments and difficulties. But Jesus never suggested that. He was compassionately present to people in their places of grief, disappointment and pain—listening to their stories, touching their sores and wounds and weeping with them in their grief. Walking with Jesus in the dark, grasping the handholds of His promises, we discover that His love is wider than our wounds, longer than our interminable winter, deeper than our loss and higher than our understanding. Hope is facing the difficult reality of what *is*, and fiercely holding on to the unchanging reality of God's presence and His promises, despite our circumstances.

Neither is biblical hope "Little Orphan Annie optimism," avoiding hard present realities by fantasizing things will get better "tomorrow." Victims of domestic violence frequently chase the fantasy that "it won't happen again." This thinking could have fatal results. Too often, Christian women rationalize denial, spiritualize insecurity and feel compelled to keep chasing fantasies and hoping against hope. But Jesus always calls us to live in the truth of what is, even if it points to an undesirable outcome. How do we do this?

On the altar of the cross, Jesus surrendered the outcome and placed His hope in God. The psalmist repeatedly says in Psalm 42 and 43, "Hope in God, for I will yet praise Him" (42:5,11; 43:5, *NLT*). Hope in—outcomes? No. Hope in God Himself, who knows the end from the beginning and holds all the seen and unseen outcomes in His hand. To hope in God means laying all the outcomes on the altar—trusting that if life doesn't go according to Plan A, God has a whole alphabet of plans. They are not His second-best plans; they are His perfect unfolding plans. Ephesians 1:11-12 says He "works out everything in conformity with the purpose of his will, in order that we, who were the first to hope in Christ, might be for the praise of his glory." God has a perfect plan from the point of your last mistake. He deftly weaves all the broken threads of our lives into His design, for our good and His glory.

When winter darkness presses in, press into God and hold fast to His Word. Mining the depths of His unfailing love and faithfulness, you will discover He Himself is your Hope.

A PLACE OF HOPE

*I would have despaired unless I had believed that I would see the goodness
of the Lord in the land of the living. Wait for the Lord; be strong and
let your heart take courage; yes, wait for the Lord.*
PSALM 27:13-14, NASB

*Why am I discouraged? Why is my heart so sad? I will put my hope
in God! I will praise him again—my Savior and my God! Now I am deeply
discouraged, but I will remember you . . . I hear the tumult of the raging
seas as your waves and surging tides sweep over me. But each day the LORD
pours his unfailing love upon me, and through each night I sing
his songs, praying to God who gives me life.*
PSALM 42:5-8, NLT

*May the God of hope fill you with all joy and peace as you trust in him,
so that you may overflow with hope by the power of the Holy Spirit.*
ROMANS 15:13

*Then Christ will make his home in your hearts as you trust in him.
Your roots will grow down into God's love and keep you strong. And may
you have the power to understand, as all God's people should, how wide,
how long, how high, and how deep his love is.*
EPHESIANS 3:17-18, NLT

FOR REFLECTION

Contrasting, dark threads in needlework create depth and dimension.
Likewise, the dark seasons of our lives can bring depth and dimension to
our relationship with God as He reveals Himself to us in profound ways.

LIVING AT A PLACE NEAR HIS ALTAR

In what aspects of life are you prone to either "Pollyanna pretending"
or "Little Orphan Anne optimism"?

In the winter of your life, where is your hope vested?

Ask God to reveal glimpses of His goodness as you walk with Him in the dark.

INVITING YOUR CHILDREN TO HIS ALTAR

Gently help your children separate wishful thinking from reality with these questions: "What makes you think so?" "Has that ever happened before?" Accept their answers as their perception of reality.

False hope creates disillusionment and disappointment. As your children live in the painful truth of what "is," offer them empathy and understanding. Remind them of God's unfailing love and His promises.

Read the Easter story (see Mark 16:1-8). How might the women have been feeling on their way to Jesus' tomb? How would remembering Jesus' promise of resurrection have changed their point of view that morning?

PRAYER NOTES AND PERSONAL REFLECTIONS

_____

_____

_____

_____

_____

_____

_____

_____

_____

_____

_____

_____

PURPOSE

Celebrating and Proclaiming God's Goodness

"I know this isn't how you would want to write the next chapter of your life, honey," I said to my daughter after her father and I separated. I wished I could tear out a few pages from the book to spare my children the spillover pain that was now part of their story. Sometimes life is just plain hard; we crane our necks and strain our eyes trying to see any of God's goodness in our circumstances. At times, a different vantage point or a different set of eyes gives us perspective. That's what I found in the heart of Africa.

Armed soldiers dotted street corners, and trucks full of U.N. peace-keeping forces rambled past amputees hobbling down the road. These were my first glimpses of life-as-usual in Burundi, a tiny, impoverished country painfully limping along in the unsteady aftermath of tribal fighting between the Hutus and Tutsis. A decade of civil war and genocide left no one untouched or unscathed; everyone had a story. Pushing through jet lag, I was on my way to church; it was Easter Sunday.

Inside the modest church building, the celebration was already underway. An electric keyboard, a couple of guitars and a drum fashioned from a metal barrel accompanied jubilant, enthusiastic singing that threatened to raise the roof. One woman on the worship team caught my eye. In the midst of energized worship, she swayed calmly on the platform. Her face was radiant as she wiped her eyes with an already shriveled tissue, reminding me of the woman who washed Jesus' feet with her tears. *What pain-filled story shaped the backdrop of her worship?* Although I could not understand her Kirundi lyrics, I was mesmerized as the message of her heart emerged in a graceful, lilting dance of pure adoration. It was Easter, and Teena celebrated resurrection from the center of her being. What was the source of her resilient hope and overflowing joy?

I had come to Burundi to teach at a women's Bible conference. Many of the women were single moms, widowed by a hideous war. As I watched their lives and listened to their tragic stories of abuse, rape and HIV, they taught me instead. During our week together, spontaneous singing, unchoreographed dancing, eager sharing of testimonies and passionate prayers marked the beginning and end of each teaching session, despite the unbearable heat and long hours of instruction. Sunday's exuberant fanfare was no mere Easter celebration; it was the joyful overflow of hearts celebrating the goodness of the One they depended on day by day. With the ever-present threat of war, peace was precarious; but in Jesus, overriding peace ruled their hearts and minds. They had experienced external bondage and oppression; but in Christ, they found unlimited inner freedom. These women had been robbed of dignity; but at the cross, they had found and claimed worth that another could never take away. They battled terminal diseases; but at the cross, they lived on the threshold of eternal life.

They had no voice, but Jesus heard their cries, and they praised Him with all their might. Basic survival was a daily struggle; God's unfailing love was their lifeline. These women lived contentedly in the moment, celebrating God's goodness. One Burundian sister emphatically declared, "Don't just say 'God is blessing me' when things are going well for you; God is blessing you ALL the time!" Eternal realities lifted their sights above their external circumstances, even as God's goodness met them *in* their circumstances, and they held fiercely to Him. This life was fragile, but every day was filled with the life-giving hope of Easter.

On the cross, Jesus authored the greatest story ever told, the story of God's goodness and love. The empty tomb reminds us that we have hope not only for the life to come, but to overcome in this life. Like our Burundian sisters, we have two stories to tell—the noticeable story of our outward set of circumstances, and the underlying story of God's life-invading, life-changing work in us. The former may be cause for heartache, but the latter gives hope—it is a cause for celebration! As we invite God to write the chapters of our lives, He invites us to participate in proclaiming and celebrating the grand unfolding story of His goodness and love!

A Place of Hope

One generation will commend your works to another; they will tell of your mighty acts. They will speak of the glorious splendor of your majesty, and I will meditate on your wonderful works. They will tell of the power of your awesome works, and I will proclaim your great deeds. They will celebrate your abundant goodness and joyfully sing of your righteousness.
Psalm 145:4-7

But we have this treasure in jars of clay to show that this all-surpassing power is from God and not from us. We are hard pressed on every side, but not crushed; perplexed, but not in despair; persecuted, but not abandoned; struck down, but not destroyed. We always carry around in our body the death of Jesus, so that the life of Jesus may also be revealed in our body. For we who are alive are always being given over to death for Jesus' sake, so that his life may be revealed in our mortal body.
2 Corinthians 4:7-11

For Reflection

Our hope rests in God's unchanging goodness and unfailing love, all the time.

Living at a Place Near His Altar

What life events have caused you to "walk with a limp"?

Do you celebrate God's goodness in all circumstances? What glimpses of His goodness can you see today?

What eternal realities can transform your view of your present circumstances?

Inviting Your Children to His Altar

Help your children see glimpses of God's goodness by asking, "What is something good that happened today?"

Pick one day each month to be "Celebration Day" to recount the ways you have seen God's goodness in your lives. A celebration can be as simple as a pancake supper or a scoop of ice cream, with candles for everyone!

Let your children participate in writing, illustrating and selecting photographs for a family log (a blank book) or family blog (online), recording stories of God's goodness throughout the year. Use this record to celebrate God's goodness to your family at Thanksgiving, when you write holiday letters or on New Year's Eve as you think back on the previous year. During difficult times, reread the family log or blog for encouragement.

PRAYER NOTES AND PERSONAL REFLECTIONS

OBEDIENCE

Daring to Live in God's Purposes

"What do you *ho-o-o-o-pe* for, what are your *dre-e-e-e-eams*, what are the *lon-n-n-ngings* God has placed within you?" the pastor prodded passionately, as if stretching out the syllables would reach deep into our souls, stirring up something that had settled in the soup of life. My pastor was leading our congregation in a Lenten series entitled "Dare to Dream." Easter was coming, and Easter meant hope. He challenged us to practice the disciplines of reading Scripture, praying and fasting, enabling us to listen to God's whisper. We were encouraged to form small groups and together dare to uncover the seeds of possibilities and purposes God had buried in our souls.

Some of us had to dig pretty deep, as hopes and dreams had been long buried under the burdens of life. The very idea of dreaming and hoping at all felt uncomfortable and risky, inviting the possibility of more disappointment in my life. And there was the rub: Our pastor was encouraging us to pull out all the stops, daring us to dream BIG and then cooperate with God in the process of bringing His purposes to fulfillment in our lives.

"Hope" in the Bible is closely tied to faith in God and daring obedience. Hebrews 11 gives us a glimpse of this. God warned Noah, and he built an ark; God called Abraham, and he got up and went straight into the unknown. God promised "good as dead" Abraham a son, and he made love to his aging, barren wife. God tested Abraham, and he passed with flying colors, keeping his eyes on God's promise. As believers, we don't hope in hope, or hope against hope; we hope in God alone.

Hope is also closely tied to the word "wait." The psalmist said he waited for the Lord "more than watchmen wait for the morning"

(Psalm 130:6). Watchmen wait actively and attentively while doing their work. Even during our waiting, we take alternating steps of faith and obedience, walking with God. During the long, dark hours of the night, the watchman knows the morning will come; it's just a matter of time. Sorrow may last for the night, but joy comes in the morning.

So during that Lenten season six years ago, I met with a small group of others who were also hoping for hope and daring to dream. We read, listened, prayed and encouraged one another as we owned our dreams. It has proven to be the most amazing journey; with each new step of faith, it seemed that God rolled out the carpet in front of me. By God's grace, each of the "hopes and dreams" I recorded came to pass over a five-year period: I earned a Master's degree; started a private counseling practice; took part in an overseas short-term mission trip; developed a writing and speaking ministry; and took part in the creation of a faith-based nonprofit agency that serves single-parent families in the community.

Some of these opportunities seemed to fall out of God's hand and right into my lap, but they didn't happen magically. They happened by prayerfully listening to Him and daring to step out in faith and obedience into the unknown. Sometimes those steps were hesitant, faltering, even stubbornly reluctant. But as I cooperated with His purposes, God walked ahead of me, weaving together the threads of unknown people and unforeseen events to produce an extraordinary tapestry. It's *His* tapestry; I am just one of the threads in His much greater design. In the center of the tapestry is the cross; at the foot of the cross is the word "hope."

Jesus went to the cross to give the hope of new life and purpose to everyone who believes and follows Him. The God of hope said, "I will lead her into the desert and speak tenderly to her there. I will return her vineyards to her and transform the Valley of Trouble into a gateway of hope" (Hosea 2:14-15, *NLT*).

What are your dreams? What do you hope for? What are the longings God has placed in your heart?

A PLACE OF HOPE

Guide me in your truth and teach me, for you are God my Savior,
and my hope is in you all day long.
PSALM 25:5

I wait for the LORD, my soul waits, and in his word I put my hope.
My soul waits for the Lord more than watchmen wait for the morning,
more than watchmen wait for the morning.
PSALM 130:5-6

The LORD delights in those who fear him, who put their
hope in his unfailing love.
PSALM 147:11

But those who hope in the LORD will renew their strength. They will soar on wings like
eagles; they will run and not grow weary, they will walk and not be faint.
ISAIAH 40:31

"For I know the plans I have for you," declares the LORD, "plans to prosper you
and not to harm you, plans to give you hope and a future."
JEREMIAH 29:11

Now faith is being sure of what we hope for and certain of what we do not see.
HEBREWS 11:1

FOR REFLECTION

Where there is God, there is hope. He is "the God of hope," who brings life out of death and transforms unhappy endings into new beginnings.

LIVING AT A PLACE NEAR HIS ALTAR

What are your hopes and dreams?

Consider forming a small group with other single moms to prayerfully explore God's purposes for your lives. Incorporate the disciplines of Scripture reading, praying, fasting and journaling to help you listen attentively to the Holy Spirit.

How are you exercising a walk of faith and obedience as you wait for God's purposes to unfold?

INVITING YOUR CHILDREN TO HIS ALTAR

As your children experience the realities of broken dreams and disappointed hopes, point them to the One who will not let them down and who will keep all of His promises to them.

Encourage your children to dream big rather than settle for mediocrity. Biographies of Christians provide great inspiration, planting seeds of faith in your children that God can use them to make a difference in the world.

Instill confidence and competence in your kids by encouraging them to set goals, identifying manageable steps to reach those goals and prayerfully supporting their efforts to achieve them. For young children, this may be as simple as setting up a lemonade stand to donate money to a local charity; for a teenager, it might be earning money for a youth retreat or a mission trip.

PRAYER NOTES AND PERSONAL REFLECTIONS

_____

_____

_____

_____

_____

_____

_____

_____

_____

_____

DAY 52

EMBRACING YOUR PLACE NEAR HIS ALTAR

At a recent gathering, the discussion question floating around the table was "What do you enjoy most about being single?" Without hesitation, I answered, "The power of choice." My mind scrolled back to my first major purchase a few weeks after my husband and I separated—a new kitchen table and chairs. I had prayed for God's provision and stumbled over the perfect kitchen set that was 80 percent off of the original price at a nearby department store, and hauled it home. It was my choice, and a good choice for my family.

The words "Needs Assembly" were daunting until I discovered the thrill of using an electric screwdriver. The power tool in my hand reminded me that I, too, was being empowered to make choices and create something new from the disassembled pieces of my life toward the end of serving and nurturing my family well. The previous chapter of our lives had ended with an unexpected, painful twist in the plot that left me reeling. Turning the pages of this new chapter of our lives, I felt extremely unsettled and very unsure of my steps. Now, each day, there were blank pages to be filled in with my own handwriting. How would I choose to shape our story?

Esther's life also took unexpected, painful twists. Her people were exiled in Babylon, and she was orphaned as a child. Later, she was drafted into King Xerxes' harem and chosen to be his queen. She did not choose these outcomes; they were foisted upon her by people and circumstances beyond her control. When the prime minister, Haman, manipulated Xerxes to issue a decree authorizing the annihilation of the Jews, Esther's cousin, Mordecai, privately challenged her to remember her identity as one of God's chosen people, embrace her position of influence and redirect the course of history for her people.

"Who knows if perhaps you were made queen for just such a time as this?" (Esther 4:14, *NLT*). Mordecai's challenge was no less than terrifying; approaching the king uninvited meant risking her life! Mordecai clearly trusted in God's sovereign power to rule and overrule in these circumstances for the sake of His people—but did Esther?

Esther could have chosen the role of a helpless victim or the convenient path of passive self-protection. Esther's remarkable response reveals a woman of humility, wisdom, courage and faith. Prayer and fasting were her immediate course of action, evidence of her humble dependence on God. What probing self-examination, pleading and fearful surrender of outcomes ensued during her three-day fast? How much time was spent in quiet listening to discern a wise plan of action that exceeded her knowledge and experience? Esther interceded for her people, and then intervened, demonstrating a holy mix of meekness of spirit and boldness of action. It was up to her; how she handled her choices now would impact everyone who depended on her.

Whatever the circumstances that resulted in us becoming single moms, we must choose how we will embrace our position "for such a time as this" in our children's lives. They are depending on us to choose wisely. Claiming our identity in Christ, and empowered by the Holy Spirit, we can make strategic choices that transform our family's story into one of hope and healing.

As we live in God's grace, we can extract valuable lessons from the past, incorporating them for good as we shape our family's future. At the foot of the cross, we can humbly surrender outcomes and faithfully apply God's truth and wisdom to the pages of our lives. By relying on His unfailing love and faithfulness, we can co-parent with God as we prayerfully intercede and courageously intervene on behalf of our children, nurturing each of them to discover and embrace their identity in Christ.

When we choose to establish our homes near His altar—the altar of the cross of Christ—we will find Him to be our sure source of security, protection, provision and blessing.

Embracing Your Place Near His Altar

I long, yes, I faint with longing to enter the courts of the Lord.
With my whole being, body and soul, I will shout joyfully to the living God.
Even the sparrow finds a home, and the swallow builds her nest and raises her young at a
place near your altar, O Lord of Heaven's Armies, my King and my God!
What joy for those who can live in your house, always singing your praises.
What joy for those whose strength comes from the Lord,
who have set their minds on a pilgrimage to Jerusalem.
When they walk through the Valley of Weeping, it will become
a place of refreshing springs.
The autumn rains will clothe it with blessings.
They will continue to grow stronger, and each of them will appear
before God in Jerusalem . . . .
For the Lord God is our sun and our shield. He gives us grace and glory.
The Lord will withhold no good thing from those who do what is right.
O Lord of Heaven's Armies, what joy for those who trust in you.
Psalm 84:2-7,11-12, *NLT*

For Reflection

"Who knows if perhaps you were made queen for just such a time as this?" To nurture your children's hearts at a place near His altar, you must daily find your own life at the foot of the cross.

Living at a Place Near His Altar

When are you tempted to fall into the role of helpless victim or take the convenient path of passive self-protection?

What are valuable lessons you can take from the past as you create a new future with your children?

How can you embrace your position of influence and choose to live at a place near God's altar in your present circumstances?

INVITING YOUR CHILDREN TO HIS ALTAR

Take your children on a nature walk, especially during springtime, to look for birds' nests. Discuss where they build their nests and the variety of materials they use to make the nest strong. Describe the ways you are building your home at a place near God's altar.

Read John 3:16. Explain how the cross of Christ became the final altar and what was the purpose of His sacrificial death. Invite your children to receive Christ as their personal Savior, if they have not done so already.

Provide age-appropriate Bibles for your children. Remind them that the Holy Spirit and the Bible are God's "power tools" to build their lives on the solid foundation of His truth, love and faithfulness.

PRAYER NOTES AND PERSONAL REFLECTIONS

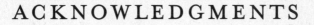

ACKNOWLEDGMENTS

I thank my heavenly Father, the Source of my identity, security and hope. When He planted the seeds of this book in my heart, He knew I'd need help along the way. He watered those seeds with the encouragement and prayers of many people to bring the project to completion.

Thanks to Cindy Oslund for telling me during my darkest days, "You're going to write a book someday," and to Karol Ladd for telling me I "*must* write." They had more confidence in me than I did and persistently coaxed and encouraged me for years before the actual writing of this book ever began.

For 24 months, a faithful community of family members and dear friends near and far have participated in this project by encircling it with prayer. My deepest thanks to my parents, Don and Ruth Grimm; my sisters, Bev Burch, Pat Baker and Rebecca Novakovich and their families; my children, Bethany Joy, Robin and Emily Floch; Angus McColl; Cindy Oslund; Karol Ladd; Brenda Smith; Sally John; Tricia Snyder; Mary Kay Gotcher; Nancy Heffner; Charlotte Seifert; Dian Stepanic; Faye Wagoner; Mike Calkin; Jackie DeRuiter; Laura Javech; Judy Harris; Rhonda Bugh; Liisa Hostetler; Sue Goldsmith; Debbie Smith; Pennie Paris; Prisca Morrison; Caroline Boykin; Amy Snedaker; Cheryl Edwards; Brenda Waggoner; Michelle Harrell; Cathy Franklin; Laura O'Connor; Claire Frost; Pam Moore; Barb Ryan; Belinda Ross; Mike Holmes; Keith Wooden; Doug Comstock; Barb Kois; Allison Lambert; Cherith Nordling; Steven Purcell; David and Beth Sutton; and Jennifer Willis. Their prayers pushed me out of the starting gate as I wrote the book proposal, petitioned God for an agent and a publisher, put wind in my sails when I was unmotivated, inspired me when I was stuck and pulled me across the finish line when deadlines approached. I am blessed beyond measure to have such a large cheering section. Only the annals of heaven will prove what their prayers accomplished, but I am quite certain the shaping and completion of this book has been a group project. My heartfelt thanks to each of them; who knew it took so many people to write a book? Only God.

Thanks to my agent, Leslie Nunn Reed, and to senior editor Steve Lawson, my editor, Kim Bangs, and others at Regal who saw the need and potential for this book and took a chance on a new author. They have all patiently answered my ignorant questions with understanding. Their words of affirmation encouraged this novice. Thanks also to my friends Anita Horton and Prisca Morrison for their personal contributions to the book.

Thanks to my parents, Don and Ruth Grimm, for their love, affirmation, encouragement and prayers. Their practical support and eager help with my children over the years have been a blessing beyond words, enabling me to pursue God's purposes unhindered.

Thanks to my daughters, Bethany Joy, Robin and Emily, for letting me include pieces of their stories in my story, for graciously accommodating this project as a factor in our lives, and for encouraging me along the way. Bethany Joy and Robin consistently inquired about my progress and cheered me on long-distance. Emily, my only daughter at home during most of the writing process, put up with less "Mom time" than usual and tolerated more leftovers than acceptable, without complaint. I owe the college girls a few care packages, and Emily a few pizzas and lots more time. Each of the girls has been a great team player over the years, and that has proven essential. I love them with all my heart and am grateful for their prayers and supportive attitudes.

To God be the glory. Great is Thy faithfulness!

To find out more about Carol Floch's writing,
speaking and counseling ministries,
visit **www.carolfloch.com**.

Carol is available to speak to women's groups,
single parent groups and recovery groups.
Please contact Carol at **carol.floch@gmail.com**.